KARL RAHNER

BELIEF TODAY

Three Theological
Meditations

translated by M. H. Heelan,
Ray and Rosaleen Ockendon, and
William Whitman

with a Preface by Hans Küng

SHEED

LONDON

Nihil obstat: Leo J. Steady, Ph.D, S.T.D, Censor

Imprimatur: † Robert F. Joyce, Bishop of Burlington, 20 June 1967

Printed in Great Britain for Sheed & Ward Ltd,
6 Blenheim Street, London W1Y 0SA by
Redwood Press Limited
Trowbridge, Wiltshire

Preface

Man's daily round of affairs is crowded with activities: we work, walk, sit, and look; we laugh, eat, and sleep. Such activities make us rich or poor. It is up to the Christian to live these activities, and yet to unlock their concealed richness and depth —in the light of Christian faith.

Belief today, the ability to believe today, means a special burden and a special grace. This holds true for every Christian, but particularly for those Christians whose mission it is to serve mankind, transmitting this faith through the Church. Christian faith today is made up of unpretentious fraternity, a reckoning with fundamental dangers, radical simplicity, and a sincere attitude toward God's otherworldliness.

Can one believe today without losing his integrity? Can the Christian who lives in today's world and who is concerned about intellectual integrity, retain his integrity in the domain of Christian faith? To answer this, we must reconsider questions which have heretofore been thought perfectly clear: what *is* intellectual integrity? what *is* Christian faith?

But we must not forget that we are not here to reflect on faith, but to live it. Wherever we find ourselves in our inquiry, the final word should and must be, "Lord, I believe, help me in my disbelief."

HANS KÜNG

Contents

BELIEF TODAY

EVERYDAY THINGS

TRANSLATED BY M. H. HEELAN

On the theology of everyday things

This is a little book of reflections on the daily round of common, ordinary things, "everyday" things—although they are most in evidence on weekdays. It is unlikely, however, that these pages will be read during the uneasy leisure of a weekday filled, as such days are, with rush and bustle and business. Rather will they be read and pondered in the peace and quiet of Sunday, that blessed day which gives us all a breathing space and respite from everyday concerns. Let us then take the opportunity that Sunday gives us and consider everyday things from an unfamiliar angle. Let us look at a few of them such as work and recreation, eating, sleeping, and so on, in the light of the Christian faith and see whether they have any significance from the standpoint of theology. Granted, of course, that even in dealing with simple things like these a few words can convey very little. And it is the simplest things too that usually give most trouble in theory and practice.

By way of introduction here are some brief general considerations.

*If your daily round seems unrewarding, don't put the blame
on it; blame yourself for not being able to evoke the riches that
are to be found in it. [Rilke.]*

In the first place, it is no purpose of our attempt at a
theology of everyday things to turn every day into a holy day.
Neither sublime faith nor eternal wisdom would render it
possible or advisable to make every day a holy day. Weekdays
and working days must remain common, ordinary, "everyday."
Only then will they be for the Christian what they ought to
be—the field for the practice of Christian principles, the
school of common sense, the training ground for patience, the
forum in which high-flown verbiage and bogus ideals are duly
deflated, the chance to see things as they really are. And this
last is surely the seed from which true wisdom will grow.

In the second place, the very commonness of everyday
things harbors the eternal marvel and silent mystery of God
and his grace and retains them only so long as it retains its
commonness. Because that commonness is the work of man,
and man, wherever he is, is the being who by his free and responsible acts unlocks the secret depths of reality. The most
common and trifling things, indeed, form part of a man's intimate personality, and as such are, or ought to be, integrated
into his life; that is, if his life is freely and firmly oriented

towards God through the faith, hope, and charity within him, and thus bears the impress of the eternal God upon it. We do not attain to God by lofty ideals or grand words or by deluding ourselves by self-flattery. God is reached by acts that strip us of our selfishness, by care for others that makes us forget ourselves, by patience that engenders serenity and wisdom. The man who, in this way, takes his tiny portion of historic time into the heart of eternity suddenly perceives that little things, too, have unutterable depths, that they are indeed heralds of eternity, always vastly greater than they seem, like drops of water that mirror the immense vault of heaven, or lowly signs that point to far-off places, or messengers dumbfounded by the news they bring of the approach of infinity, or like shadows of true being cast across our path because being itself is almost upon us.

This brings us to our third point. On Sundays we should be kind to the homely little things of every day. After all they only irritate us if they turn up when we are already annoyed. They only bore us when we fail to grasp their significance and only press us down into the rut when we misunderstand and mishandle them. They have the power, too, to make us sensible and clearheaded, weary and frustrated—but also humble, quiet, and resigned. And is not this just what we ought to be? That is a lesson hard to learn but learn it we must. It is a necessary prelude to our presence at the eternal banquet to be prepared for us not by human hands but by the grace of God.

Lastly, these little everyday things should never make us bitter and spiteful sceptics. The little is the promise of the great, and time is the embryo of eternity, and this holds good for weekdays as well as Sundays.

On work

Work is, of course, the characteristic feature of what we call our working day or weekday. There are people who surround it with a halo and hymn its praises as the expression of the great and glorious creative ability of mankind in the mass. Some misuse it also (and how often, too!) as a means of escape from themselves, from the secret and mystery of their own being, from that anguish which torments them in their strivings after objective certainty. But the true sense of work is to be found somewhere between these aberrations. It is neither the highest and noblest thing in life nor the drug prescribed to deaden the impact on man of the mystery of his existence. It is just work, that's all, a tiresome thing but tolerable enough, nothing to make a fuss about, for it comes round regularly with the clock. It sustains life on the one hand and wears life out on the other. It is a thing that cannot be avoided, but when it does not deteriorate into unbearable drudgery, it can be reasonable and friendly.

Work never comes quite natural to us. Even when it starts out briskly to give effect to our highest creative impulses, it has the habit of lapsing into the jog trot of dull, repetitive routine. It is perpetually plagued, too, with the need to make provision for the unexpected and for the drawback that what a person does not do from inner incentive but under compulsion from outside and at the behest of strangers, he merely puts up with; his heart is not in it. Moreover, work requires the activity of the individual worker to be coordinated with the activities of the group and subjected to the regulation of a given rhythm; the work of each is a contribution to a common objective which, however, no individual worker has personally chosen. This calls for obedience and self-denial all round.

The first thing, then, that theology has to say about work is simply that it is, and will continue to be, work, tiresome and monotonous and involving the surrender of the worker's will to the demands of the daily round. As time goes on work may become more and more productive as the result of new ideas and inventions, but, so far as man is concerned, its limits are fixed by biological factors which impel him steadily and inexorably towards the grave. Work always has reciprocal relations with the world outside the workshop; they tend to be unstable, for the outside world can never be brought under complete control. And so work is likely to remain work, and to continue to be as Holy Writ described it—a sign of the fallen state of mankind, a sign of the disharmony between what is within us and what outside, between freedom and necessity, flesh and spirit, the individual and society; and this disharmony can be overcome only by God's grace.

The phenomenon of sin, which is the result of this disharmony, gave rise in Christ (who was, of course, sinless) to the phenomenon of bodily redemption. Christ delivered us not only from death, the most radical effect of our fall, but from every other outward sign of our separation from God. In this way he has delivered us also from the tiresomeness, drabness, and (virtual) depersonalization of work. Through the grace of Jesus Christ, therefore, and not through any merit inherent in itself, work, when "done in the Lord," helps to form in us the attitude and disposition which God desires in those he invites to his eternal feast: that patience by which we can bear everyday witness to our faith, that faithfulness and detachment which spring from the Christian sense of responsibility, and that unselfishness which is the very food of love.

On getting about

Getting about is one of our most common everyday activities, so common that we never give it a thought until something turns up which restricts or prohibits the use of our legs. Then the ability to get about suddenly becomes a wonderful boon, a heaven-sent blessing. Human beings, unlike plants, are not tied to a circumscribed environment. They can seek out an environment for themselves, decide to change it, choose another and—off they go. The feeling of freedom that this ability to get about gives us is evident even as we go on our daily round, despite the fact that the direction of our steps is dictated by the demands of the job. All this going about breeds in us the spirit of the roamer, the seeker, who does not know where he is going, much less when he will get there. A time comes, however, when we feel we want to make for a definite goal and not just wander about aimlessly.

We sometimes speak of a "walk" or "way" of life. Now we find in Holy Writ that Christians were at first known as those "belonging to the Way." (Acts ix.2.) When the Bible wishes to impress on us that we should not only listen to the word of God but practice it, it tells us that we must not only live in the Spirit, but "walk" in the Spirit. Again, one of the most time-honored elements in public celebrations, secular as well as religious, is a procession. Man's life, too, is often described as a pilgrimage, and a pilgrimage certainly connotes an uncommon amount of getting about.

These are a few indications (there are many more) that our lives have long been likened to the primitive, natural, everyday phenomenon of getting about. And this purely physical activity of continually moving from one place to another warns us that we have here no sure abode. We are still wayfarers heading for a destination but uncertain of the way, pilgrims, wanderers between two worlds, beings in transition, borne along by some external power, but retaining the ability to guide and direct our course. We do not always succeed, however, in reaching the destinations we plan for ourselves.

We see, therefore, that the progress of a free and responsible human being as he goes on his everyday round typifies man's whole existence. His faith reveals to the Christian the goal of his existence and assures him he will reach it. He is borne along incessantly by some power conscious of itself and of not having fulfilled its purpose, a power ever seeking, ever believing it will find its goal in the end, because (and how could it be otherwise?) that goal is God himself towards whose Second Coming, in the person of Christ, our own future moves inexorably.

So we have to keep on getting about, to keep on seeking our

goal. The Holy One, for his part, will come and look for us if we only go towards him, walk in his way. When we have found him—or rather when he has found us—we shall learn that our meeting had already been determined by the power that bore us on towards God, and that the stirring of that power within us was the sign that God had come to meet us. And that power is what we call God's grace.

On sitting down

Sitting down certainly belongs to the realm of the ordinary and so is another subject for our theology of everyday things. Who has never gladly and gratefully dropped into a chair after a spell of hard work or a day in the open air? Even a roving disposition does not inhibit an occasional inclination to sit and rest awhile. And everybody will agree that one must sit down when something especially worthwhile crops up in the course of one's work. Sitting down also demonstrates that in the biological and terrestrial domain every place and every posture is not of equal value. For a person belongs *somewhere* and cannot be equally at home *anywhere*; his ultimate aim is to settle down and "take root." All his comings and goings can be regarded indeed as simply the outward expression of his inward yearning for some place where he can make a home, establish a "seat" (not necessarily a country mansion) and lead a really full life at last.

It is obvious, of course, that sitting, in the physical sense, reflects only one side of human existence and its fulfillment. It neither affirms nor denies that rest invariably follows on the heels of achievement or that man always finds a spot where he can settle down at last and take his rest. (Which of us indeed can be sure of the eternal rest that is eternal life?) But sitting down somehow suggests tranquillity, the inward joy that comes from possessing, without fear of loss, the things that endure, the things of the spirit. It also implies the absence of aimless activity.

The Gospel, speaking of the banquet of eternal life, says: "The master . . . will . . . have them sit. . . ." (Luke xii. 37.) A peaceful and innocent scene, surely, but we may ask in all seriousness whether we have the strength of mind, integrity and independence of spirit to sit down and rest occasionally, or whether we are the sort of people who must always be up and doing, always in the thick of things, because we simply cannot bear peace and quiet. Are we, too, always running about in an effort to run away from ourselves? Do we think of Sunday as just another kind of working day, a break in the everyday round dictated by purely physiological considerations?

It is time we learned that rest can be a higher form of activity, activity of the mind and spirit and, therefore, activity of the whole man. In the long run, indeed, it is the only form of such activity. It is time we pressed the view that people are not dispensed from reading signposts because they happen to be fast drivers, and that slower travellers often arrive sooner because they have given some thought to their goal and how to reach it. Better a steady movement towards one's goal than premature eternal rest caused by overacceleration! We should aim at acquiring this habit of steady, deliberate advance towards our objective. The first and most essential step is to give up thinking that futile, self-escaping activity is better and more bearable than rest and reflection.

There are plenty of ways by which the habit of calm and quiet reflection can be cultivated. We can, for example, learn to appreciate good works of art, good music, and the higher pleasures of the mind, for their own sake. There are so many artistic and intellectual experiences which help to make a whole man! We can look around us now and then and marvel at the depth and unselfishness of the love that one human being can have for another. Humanity, after all, is worth looking at, we are pledged to love our neighbor.

And, finally, there is the abiding peace of prayer. Only in loving union with that infinite mystery whom we call God can man attain that ultimate goal beyond which he cannot go. There he will find rest that is not just a short halt in his erratic journey. There he will hear the words for which all sitting and resting are only symbols and promises: "He who conquers, I will grant him to sit with me on my throne." (Rev. iii.21.)

On seeing

Seeing is, of course, one of those basic functions that are in-dispensable to us day in and day out. We do not propose to inquire here into its aspects as a physiological and epistemo-logical phenomenon. It is certainly our most objective and positive method of contact with the world we live in. It opens up to us the widest possible prospect, it brings distant objects closer and causes nearer ones to stand out more clearly. It puts objects, as it were, in their proper place, distinguishes between them and relates them to one another. It forms them into a world full of beauty and variety.

But the eye is also—and we have the Bible's word for it—the window in which its owner is on view; it is the gateway through which the outside world streams in to him and the gateway through which he goes out from the secret places of his inner being to the outside world. The Bible tells us, too, that his eye reveals a man's anxiety, yearning, pride, pity, goodness, wickedness, ill will, scorn, envy and deceit. And the Bible also makes the eyes stand for the outward aspect of man, that which the world sees, while God sees into the inmost recesses of man's heart which no man can penetrate. In this way the seeing, outward-looking eye becomes a sort of central point or point of meeting between internal and external, between man and the world; it gathers in, on the one hand, and dispenses, on the other; it reveals but yet conceals.

It would be too much for us in this short essay to go into the intricate analogies between seeing-and-hearing and man's encounter with God and Christ, which are to be found in some religious writing. We shall keep to the theme of seeing in its everyday sense. That shows us, well enough, man as he is and as he ought to be if he is to become a whole man. Every day we meet the bluff and hearty man, the shrewd and cautious man, and the man whose eyes are fixed on far-off and unattainable things.

But how rarely do we come across a man courageous and candid enough to show his real self and speak his own mind and let others know him for what he really is! Such a man looks out upon the world and sees it in a true light; he dares to look it straight in the face and does not superimpose another, and wishful, image upon its homely features. And he does not fabricate a double image of himself by separating appearance from reality; he comes before the world in his true colors. Such a man is clear-eyed; the eye of his inner being is sound. As he goes upon his daily round his eye reflects the image and likeness of the right and proper "outlook on the

world," the only true *Weltanschauung*. To him we can apply
the words of Jesus in the Sermon on the Mount: "The eye is
the lamp of the body. So, if your eye is sound, your whole
body will be full of light." (Matt. vi.22.)

On laughter

The daily round brings not only serious work but also—let us hope—occasional laughter. Laughter itself has its serious side. It often betrays us better than words do. By laughter we mean sane, wholesome laughter and rule out the laughter of fools and sinners, such as that mentioned by the wise Sirach (Ecclus. xxi.23; xxvii.14) and that which our Lord promised would come to a bad end. (Luke vi.25.) The laughter we are concerned with is that spontaneous laughter that wells up from a gay and innocent heart. Such laughter comes only from someone who loves his kind and has a ready, almost instinctive, fellow feeling for them all, singly and in the mass. Such a person is likely to take a sane view of circumstances and situations and make an appropriate response. He will treat big things in a big way and little things with a light touch; he will take serious matters seriously and laugh at funny things. For all these things happen in the way God meant them to, and they should be taken that way; and where they tickle our sense of humor they are fit subjects for laughter.

Not everybody, however, has a genuine sense of humor. That calls for an altruistic detachment from oneself and a mysterious sympathy with others which is felt even before they open their mouths. Only the person who has also a gift for affection can have a true sense of humor. A good laugh is a sign of love; it may be said to give us a glimpse of, or a first lesson in, the love that God bears for every one of us.

But this innocent, harmless laughter of the children of God is even more than that. It is also an image of something else. Holy Writ mentions the analogy we have in mind. We surely have a right to expect this little creature called laughter to lapse suddenly into silence and nothingness when it enters the eternal halls of heaven. The Bible corrects that impression; it actually makes laughter the image and likeness of God's feelings towards what goes on here below. A startling statement, indeed! But the Bible says that God laughs in heaven with the laugh of the carefree, the secure and unthreatened, the laugh of divine superiority over all the cruel, bloodstained, agonizing, insane disorder that characterizes the history of the world; it tells us that he goes on laughing, unruffled—one might almost say unmoved—as he looks down indulgently upon the lamentable spectacle spread out below him. (Is he not entitled to do so? Did not his own eternal word weep with us and suffer all the misery that man can suffer when God forsakes him?)

God laughs, says the Bible. When the last piece of human

folly makes the last burst of human laughter ring out crisp and clear in a doomed world, is it too much to imagine that this last laugh will resemble that of God, glorious and triumphant, and seem to convey that, in spite of everything, all's well?

On eating

There seems to be no end to what we hear and read about the chemico-physiological aspect of eating and drinking. Meanwhile we are in danger of coming to regard these activities as just so much refilling or "tanking up" of our bodily machine with physical energy in order to keep it going for another spell. But where man really eats and doesn't merely feed, like the animals, eating is an affair of the whole man, and when it ceases to be so, its physiological process is invariably upset.

Eating may be an everyday activity but it is no less mysterious for that. In fact, there is hardly anything in our daily experience more shrouded in mystery than the process of nutrition, the transformation of dead matter into living matter, the conversion of extraneous material into our own bodily tissues, the absorption of one being by a higher and more complex being for the sustenance of the latter. Only someone who thinks that life is just a complicated mechanical combination of chemical and physical elements can fail to marvel at such a metamorphosis. What is more, the nutritional process in man transforms food into *human* stuff, that is into a being that reflects upon itself, is present to itself, is master of itself, and in which the world becomes conscious of itself. If, ultimately, the lower can be envisaged only in terms of the higher (and not vice versa, as superficial thinkers are prone to believe), then we can say that eating is the lowliest, although the most fundamental, form of a process (the nutritional process) whose noblest product is a rational being who gives himself lovingly and unreservedly to the whole environment or world which his awareness presents to him.

It is understandable, therefore, that if the greater and higher aspects of man's being—those things which make him greater and higher than other beings—are to be symbolized in tangible form, the eating of a meal will be the favored symbol. And what better way is there of symbolizing—or even actually bringing about—a loving, confiding unity among men than eating together, all sharing in common that bodily nourishment essential to their common existence, and all, in the course of this, opening their hearts to one another? But a meal can stand also as a sign for the final and perfect communion of humanity that will take place at the eternal banquet where the bread that will be eaten and the cup that will be drunk will be the Lord himself. Then indeed will men be truly united to one another and to God.

And so, wherever we take a meal—even a weekday one—there should be a festive touch about it. This is the way in which we can make every day a feast day. For our meal proclaims the unity in which we long to merge ourselves, in which each of us will be set free from the prison of his loneliness. On weekdays perhaps the proclamation will be *sotto voce*, but it should be audible enough for us to grasp that it is a reminder of the banquet of eternal life to which we are all invited.

On sleep

We sleep away a good third of our lives. Sleep is, therefore, as much an everyday occupation as the more active employments of our waking hours. Is there a theology of sleep, too? Most certainly! In the first place the word of God confirms in a wonderfully human way our own experience of sleep. It speaks of the good sleep that follows a day's work well done, the lack of sleep of the person who brings his worries to bed with him, the sleep of the sluggard who slumbers long and late, and the like. The Bible also finds in sleep the image and likeness of something more serious; it is an image of death, of the deadly gloom of despair, of that degradation which is the effect of sin. Sleep is also represented in the Bible as a time when man's inner being is relaxed and he is susceptible to God's prompting (for the Lord reveals himself in sleep) and to significant dreams that, on the one hand, may spring from the memory of experiences buried deep in his subconsciousness, but, on the other hand, may embody the promptings and behests of God.

As a matter of fact our night's sleep is a very mysterious thing. Man, a free person and his own master and guide, lets go of himself in sleep, loses control of himself, commits himself to the powers of his own unconscious self which he has not brought into existence and does not understand. Sleep is an act of confidence in the inherent rightness, security, and goodness of man's world, an act of faith and acquiescence in what is beyond one's control.

So we realize that sleep is not at all a dull stupor induced by physiological causes; it is an act of our whole being entered into consciously and confidently. When we pray, too, we commit our being consciously and confidently to God and place it at his disposal in token of our love. No wonder Christ felt that sleep should be prefaced with an evening prayer. In our own evening prayer we must ask God to cleanse us of our sins and reconcile us with himself; we can then safely take leave of the day and its doings and confide ourselves to his loving care.

As we glide into the dark depths of our own being, no harm can then befall us; they are already blest. No angel of darkness will be there to disturb our night's rest, but the angels of God will watch over and protect it. Our sleep will be peaceful and relaxed, open to the promptings of eternal truth on which all free personality and all man's plans must be firmly grounded if man is to be, and to remain, sound in mind and spirit.

On grace in everyday life

Has any of us ever really felt that God's grace was working within him? By grace we do not mean pious sentiments of one kind or another, or that sort of religious uplift occasionally experienced on Sundays and holy days, or that faint feeling of consolation which steals over us now and then in time of trouble. We mean the real, genuine experience of a visitation of the Holy Spirit, third person of the Blessed Trinity, who was manifested to us through Christ's incarnation and sacrifice on the cross. Can man experience grace at all in this life? If he could not, surely there would be an end to our faith, an end to that holy twilight which envelops us all through our earthly pilgrimage? Now the mystics tell us—and attest it by the example of their lives—that they have had experience of God and, therefore, of grace. The experiential knowledge of God through mysticism is, however, a dim mysterious thing that one cannot discuss if one has not had it and one does not discuss if one has experienced it. Our initial question, accordingly, does not admit of a simple a priori answer.

Perhaps, however, there are degrees in the experience of grace and perhaps the lowest of these are accessible to us. First let us ask ourselves whether we have ever had experience of the working of the spiritual, or *spirit*, in man. (What we mean here by "spirit" is itself not easy to explain in a few words: we shall return to this.) To such a question one might reply, perhaps, somewhat on the following lines. "Of course I realize that man has a higher—spiritual—side to his nature; I feel it in myself every day. I think, study, make decisions, transact business, cultivate relations with other people, live in a society based not on physical subsistence alone but also on the needs of the mind and what I would call the spirit. I love, enjoy myself, appreciate poetry and can find my way about the good things of culture, science, art, and so on. Surely I can be said to know something about the working of the spirit in man?"

All this is true, to be sure, but the answer is not quite as simple as that. In every one of the activities mentioned the so-called "spirit" is (or could be) only the ingredient, so to speak, that brightens life and gives some meaning to it. The spirit in its own unique transcendence need not be present in any of them. This does not mean to say that the spirit is present as such only when we happen to be talking or philosophizing about its transcendence. On the contrary. If that were so it might be only a derived and secondary experience, for the spirit only manifests itself as an *inner* impulse in our lives. But where or how (one might ask) is real experience of the spirit to be had? And at this point we should feel it was high time to say: "Let us see whether the spirit has been at work in our own lives. There, perhaps, we may be able, with due diffidence and caution, to indicate a number of cases in point."

Can we recall any occasion when we kept silent although we longed to defend ourselves and although we were in danger of being unjustly dealt with? Did we ever freely forgive someone from whom nothing was expected in return and who would take our silent forgiveness simply as a matter of course? Did we ever obey, not because to do otherwise would have got us into trouble, but solely for the sake of those silent, incomprehensible mysteries which we call God and God's will? Did we ever make a sacrifice that was thankless and unnoticed and did not even give us a sense of inner satisfaction? Were we ever a prey to utter loneliness? Did we ever decide on something purely at the dictates of our own conscience, something that could not be discussed with or explained to anybody else. Something in which we acted entirely on our own, fully aware that we were taking a step for whose consequences we should be held everlastingly accountable?

Have we ever tried to persevere in the love of God when all emotion and enthusiasm had deserted us, when we could no longer mistake our own doings and impulses for manifestations of God's will; when it seemed as if God's love would be the death of us, when we could see in it only the renunciation of everything, life as well as all else; when our prayer seemed to be uttered into the empty, unanswering void and when the bottomless depths of a dreadful abyss seemed to be opening before us; when everything seemed to be incomprehensible and devoid of all meaning? Have we ever performed a duty that could only be carried out under circumstances which forced us to deny and forget ourselves, or in circumstances that involved doing some outrageously stupid and thankless thing? Did we ever do a kindness to a person from whom we could not expect as much as a shadow of gratitude or appreciation, while at the same time we had not even the compensation of feeling we had acted unselfishly or decently in doing so?

Let us look into our lives, then, and see if we can discover whether any such experience ever came our way. If we find it did, we may be sure that the spirit was at work within us then, and eternity and ourselves had a brief encounter; that the spirit means more than an ingredient in the make-up of a transient world, and the significance of man is not of the same order as the significance of this world or worldly happiness; that certain hazards can be faced with an unbounded confidence quite unconnected with worldly results.

From all this we can form an idea of the secret longing for the spirit that is felt by truly spiritual persons, the saints in particular. Again and again these are racked by the anxiety to make sure that they have really done with the world and have begun to live in the spirit. They have tasted the sweetness of the spirit. To the ordinary run of men such experiences would be only embarrassing, though perhaps, unavoidable, interruptions in the real business of life; or else the spice and trimmings of another (abnormal!) kind of life that had somehow strayed into their own down-to-earth existences. But truly spiritual people get the true unadulterated sweetness of the spirit. They have drunk the spirit of life neat, so to speak; they have imbibed it in the true sense of the word, instead of merely enjoying it as a relish spread over their earthly career.

That explains the remarkable lives of the saints, their poverty, the humility by which they set great store, their yearning for death, their readiness to suffer, and their intense, secretly cherished desire for martyrdom. All this is not to say that they are free from human weaknesses, or to deny that every now and then they have to come down from the heavenly heights to the level of every day. They know well that God's grace can also bless the dull round of daily tasks well done, and bring the doers a step nearer to God. They know, too, that we earthbound creatures are not angels and were never meant to be. But they realize that man, inasmuch as he is a spiritual being, is really and truly (and not just theoretically) standing midway between God and the world, between time and eternity, and they are so certain of this that they are constantly trying to make their lives such that the spirit within them shall not be just the ingredient that supplies such refinement as there is in human existence.

When we Christians, living by faith, experience the action of the spirit, it means that we are, in point of fact, having contact with the *supernatural*, although the contact may be scarcely perceptible. Indeed it may be that we cannot, or should not, directly confront it. But when, on such occasions, our

inner being seems for perhaps one brief moment to escape
from our control; when everything tangible and describable
and perceptible seems to recede into the background of our
awareness; when, after a deathlike silence, loud noises ring
out; when we seem to taste nothing but death and destruction
about us; or when everything seems to vanish into an ineffable,
pervasive, impalpable bliss—then we may be sure it is not only
the human spirit but the Holy Spirit himself that is working
within us. That is our moment of grace, the moment when,
from his boundless infinity which for us is so close to nothingness, God, tremendous and unfathomable, enters into communion with us.

When, therefore, we no longer cling to self or even pay
attention to it; when we deny ourselves in serving others;
when we view our own selves and everything else as objects
far away in the infinite distance—then we are at last beginning
to live in the world of God, the God of grace and of life ever-
lasting. But we cannot do this all at once; we shall often be
tempted in the early days of our new life to fly back in alarm
to the refuge of familiar things and familiar ways, and who
will blame us if we do? But we should try, nevertheless, to
get accustomed, by degrees, to the taste of the pure spiritual
wine which is filled with the Holy Spirit. And we should
never, on any account, push away the chalice that his provi-
dence and will hold out to us.

In this life the chalice of the Holy Spirit is identical with
the chalice of Jesus Christ. It is drunk only by those who have
slowly and with difficulty learnt to discern the fullness that

is in emptiness, the sunrise in sunset, the life in death, the self-discovery in self-renunciation. They who learn to do this experience the working of the spirit, the real spirit, the Holy Spirit of grace. For this freeing of the spirit from its earthly fetters can be fully and finally accomplished only through the grace of Christ working upon faith. And when the spirit is freed by supernatural grace, it is freed in order that it may enter into the life of God himself.

Let us then search our own lives for instances of God's grace, but not in order to boast when we have found any. God's grace cannot be found in the sense that lost property is found; it cannot be reclaimed triumphantly into our own possession. It can only be found in seeking God and surrendering ourselves to him in self-abandoning love, unconditionally and for ever. We should continue to ask ourselves as we go through life whether we feel that we are being granted this favor of living by dying to ourselves. Such self-examination is a good measure of how far we have to go before we can hope to encounter the Holy Spirit in our own so-called spiritual life. *Grandis nobis restat via. Venite et gustate, quam suavis sit Dominus!* A long road may still lie ahead of us but let us accept the Holy Spirit's invitation given through the inspired psalmist: "O taste and see that the Lord is good!"

II FAITH TODAY

TRANSLATED BY RAY AND ROSALEEN OCKENDON

Faith for today

We are all priests, we are all of us a "royal priesthood" (1 Pet 2:9). So the subject of this meditation is one which concerns every Christian. And the more a Christian feels a priestly responsibility for his brethren, the more it is his concern. But it is important most of all, and in a very special way, for the man whose calling and vocation it is to serve his fellow men in the Church through the preaching of the word and the giving of the sacraments. The burdens and cares of every believer are, indeed must be, his special burdens and cares. The strength and consolation which every believer finds can be his special strength and consolation.

It may be useful to start with three observations which both justify and delimit our reflections on this theme.

Firstly, faith of its very nature has a constantly changing historical form. So we can speak in a truly essential sense of faith today, and not only in the sense that the same faith must be practised in different historical situations external to that faith. For a Christian this needs no explanation: he is familiar with the history of revelation and hence with the history of faith, even though there is only one salvation which in any age depends on one unchanging faith as a basis of the relationship between God and man. Paradoxically, God's call to man has a history *because* it is always the same call: the evolution is in man's response to this call through the ages; and since the changes in man's response are conditioned and caused by the nature of God's call, it is a history of that call too: the history of revelation and of faith in one.

The history of faith is not completed simply because revelation came to an end eschatologically in Christ. For this ending is only an ending in so far as it marks (properly understood) the beginning of the direct self-revelation of God, occurring explicitly in the words of the prophets and apostles of Christ. So faith in Jesus Christ is not just the acceptance by more and more people in an identical and immutable way of the infinite eschatological message. Nor is it accompanied merely by an external, historical reflection upon faith, known as the history of theology. Faith has a history of its own, because the absolute self-revelation of God, addressed to the individual, necessarily includes the unlimited possibility of acceptance in a variety of ways by finite subjects. The acceptance of the message is in itself a free gift of God's grace, given to each individual and each epoch in a different fashion. The theological reflection upon the acceptance of the message is itself part of that acceptance, so that the actual history of theology is necessarily both a part of and a reflection of the actual history of faith.

The eschatological *kairos* of Christ is absolute fulfillment and total revelation; the history of Christianity in that *kairos*, in the fullness of time which has already been fulfilled, is only meaningful if in these "last days" there can be and is a true history of faith, that is, if our faith, while remaining the same unique faith, constantly undergoes a change in form. Neither God nor man are content to repeat themselves. History is not a string of repetitions, each with its place in time, but the uniqueness of a single event already present in its unchanging essence, yet constantly seeking its identity because only in this way can it renew and fulfill itself. The same is true also of the faith of the Church after the time of Christ. It has to discover a new form for each individual and for every age in order to remain true to the primitive faith. Hence nobody can believe without adding to the faith of his spiritual ancestors. Every one has to come to his own faith in a new and different way from others before him, if he wants it (as *fides qua* and *fides quae*) to be a real, living, present-day form of the primitive faith.

From this we can see that we are right to ask ourselves in all seriousness what exactly faith today is. Of course, reflection upon the form of this faith of the Christian and priest today can never be an adequate reflection of it. For the person involved the historically unique form of his action is part of the action itself, not of the reflection upon it. The latter can be better carried out by others rather than by the man involved who is unaware of all the implications of his actions. Future generations will be far more capable than we are of saying what our faith was like, since it will have influenced their own. But if reflection, however imperfect, is always an element in the action itself and if, conscious of its shortcomings, it is really to entrust itself to the mysterious purpose of God, then we can, indeed must, ask what our faith is today, before we can realise it to the full as we are bound to do. In doing so we must not, however, lose sight of the fact that ultimately it is impossible for us to act and reflect at one and the same time.

Secondly, the history of faith shows that it does not enter the same new phases in all cultures, civilisations, and individuals at one and the same time. On the contrary, the most diverse forms of faith can coexist, just as we find side by side at the same time widely differing cultures, levels of education, social classes, movements of ideas, national characteristics—in short, all those different aspects of life which condition the history of faith and of which it is a part. Thus if we try to say something about the form of our faith today, we cannot expect to describe all the varieties of faith among all our contemporaries. A Sicilian and a German, a man of seventy and a man of thirty, a European and an African Christian, the southern European with his static and orthodox views and the northern Catholic with his necessarily "Protestant" outlook, the modern scientific man and the man who lives largely untouched by science, the primitive countryman and the city-dweller in the environment of a technological mass culture—these and many other types of men live at the same time in history but clearly they live the one Christian and Catholic faith in many different ways and forms. It is not my purpose here to embark on a typology of the different modes of faith.

So if we speak of the form of faith today, we are starting from a given situation which does not apply to everyone equally. What I have to say, therefore, will apply to only one section of the faithful, and it will hardly be suprising if it arouses no echoes in the minds of many and offers them no help or inspiration. I can only hope that the form of faith that I am about to describe does at least exist and that, for a not insignificant number of people living in the typical Western European situation, it may be of importance to recognize this form as their own.

My third point is that a believer does not necessarily possess, simply because he believes and is a man of good will, the form of faith which is most suitable for him. No, the form of faith proper to a particular historical situation, for all that it is a grace given to us, is also an act which is demanded of us and which we can fail to perform. Faith, even where it has been granted, may not find the form most suited to a particular age, culture, individual or historical situation, or may find it only partly or imperfectly. For example, where in a given historical situation the most apt form of faith would be an open one, exposing itself to this situation, accepting its challenges and acting as a leaven in its midst, it can through fear turn out to be a ghetto-faith of timid conservatism, of sullen resentment, of arrogant self-satisfaction, of bigotry, of parochial narrow-mindedness, and so on.

Faith can fail to achieve the form demanded of it, and the believer may lack sufficient courage to change himself and accept new forms; instead he clings to forms which were once valuable but are now ineffective and meaningless, he will not abandon the condemned mentality of a dying era but sees it as the only climate suited to faith, he banishes from his mind all that belongs to the mentality of a new age. Faith such as this is threatened more surely than if it were exposed to the dangers of a change of form; its witness is unconvincing and ineffectual. For this reason it is of vital importance to become aware of the forms of faith demanded of us today, here and now. If we refuse to do this in theory and in practice, then (and this runs counter to the whole nature of Christian faith) we are living a form of faith which is condemned by history to disappear and which will involve faith itself in its destruction, in so far as men contribute to the rise or the decline of Christian witness.

After these preliminary remarks my intention is to present some of the characteristics of the form of faith we need today as simply as possible, without putting them into categories. I am aware that on the one hand these characteristic features of faith today take their origin from the nature of faith itself and may therefore be regarded as features of faith in any age. On the other hand certain features become more apparent at certain times and may not always be so marked at others. They belong therefore to the form of faith today as such and may not be understood and achieved by everyone to the same degree in this historical context.

The "proof" (in general only an incidental proof) of what follows lies therefore in the fact that my thesis rests simultaneously on the permanent essence of faith and on its particular temporal characteristics, which are an essential part of the form of faith today. These characteristics will only be appreciated in full by one who has been granted by God, to a greater extent than other men, the task and the opportunity, the burden and the grace, of truly living in this "today" from which the future of history will be born. Such a man is not superior to others, but different from them; and the difference is a real one whether it is recognized or—as usually happens—ignored or disputed.

Fraternal faith

The first characteristic of faith today I should like to stress can be summed up in one word: brotherly. What do I mean by that? The word implies a realtionship, refers the individual to another person, whom he should regard as his brother. Christian brotherly love implies that in the exercise of his faith the priest in particular should approach his fellow men as brothers, and that this relationship, consciously and existentially, should form a part of his faith today. The "brother" in question is first of all the layman, and then any man, even one who does not think he believes, indeed even one who rejects faith.

This relationship, whether consciously achieved or not, belongs primarily to the nature of faith and above all to the nature of the faith of a priest. Christian faith is in fact, whether we realise it or not, an essential link with the Church, with the "faithful." It is fundamentally the acceptance of

God's message, in which, quite apart from his unique call to each individual, God addresses his spiritual creatures as a whole, establishes a kingdom, a union which embraces mankind as a whole, and then manifests himself to each individual, communicating his message through the agency of man. Faith both presupposes the community and creates it; the courage to believe is always born of a pentecostal event, where many are gathered together in unity of purpose. Faith is our confidence in the personal experience of others, a conviction gained through the power of the Spirit which is at work in others, our personal experience of the Spirit given to us for the sake of others. This permanent characteristic of faith which I have sketched out should be one of the most notable characteristics of the form of faith today. It cannot be sufficiently stressed, however, that this brotherly love is not directed towards an abstract but towards our actual brother here and now, our "neighbor."

In fact we priests, in particular, run the unspoken and unconscious danger—a danger which for that reason is all the more real, ineradicable, and fateful—of believing that we have a different faith from the layman. Naturally we don't consciously believe this in theory, but we constantly run the risk of living as though it were so. And today it is more difficult than it ever was to reconcile such an attitude with the real faith that is in us and in the other members of the Church. Of course, we are God's messengers, heralds of his mysteries. But because of this we easily forget the real meaning of faith: that we are first and foremost believers like all the rest, be-

lievers with all the burdens, risks, dark hours, and temptations
that faith involves, and the need constantly to achieve it anew.

Without meaning to, we think or act as though we were
God's magistrates or the civil servants in his government of
the world. We see ourselves as God's experts and unconsciously it is ourselves that we are defending when we think
we are defending or spreading the Church of God's work of
salvation. We often act as though we had a private view of
God's plans, as though everything were clear to us, whereas
others had better merely do what we tell them since we are
the experts in heavenly affairs. This is why we often fail to
engage in real dialogue with other Christians, why we are often
not genuinely convinced that we can learn from them, from
their faith and their crises of faith.

Today our faith must be a faith of brotherliness. It must
be humble; it is only a real faith when it is not that of the
beati possidentes. We must truly share our faith with others,
put ourselves in the ranks of those who believe with difficulty
and in spite of temptation, those who wonder what they really
mean when they repeat the formulas of faith, those who ask
what these formulas have to do with the real business of living,
those who are tortured by the nagging suspicion that the edi-
fice of faith is nothing more than a traditional superstructure
—covering up other attitudes which really control their lives
—because they are unwilling to admit publicly what they
really feel.

If we have a fraternal faith, we will not masquerade as what
we are not, we will not bear witness to anything we are not

carrying out or trying to carry out in practice in our lives, painfully and prayerfully; fraternal faith means a daily struggle against the routine of the theological terms and countless moral recipes we have learned and continue to hand on to others often without having fully understood them. Theology is good, necessary, and we shall never have finished studying it. Yet how second-rate theological subtlety is where real problems are concerned, when compared with the qualities of mind or heart which we will have to rely on to solve the ultimate questions of faith. At this level we priests have no advantage over the laity.

Let us be to ourselves and to the layman what we are: men who seek, who ask, who are tempted and are filled with anxiety, just as they are; men who pray: "Lord, I believe; help my unbelief!" Let us not playact steadfastness and serenity of faith if we do not possess them. Let us not pretend that we find everything in the world of faith equally important or equally easy to put into practice with equal fervour, simply because it is all part of God's revelation. Our brothers, the laity, are unable to do this, and we shouldn't pretend that we can manage it. We may not be selective in our formal assent, in some cases only implicit, to the things revealed by God and taught by the Church with absolute authority. But as regards the things which we put into practice explicitly and existentially, the things by which we live and to which our lives bear witness, then we can and must distinguish between degrees of concern, of practice, of intensity of witness. Let us believe as our brothers in the Church do. Let us put our trust in the fact that we as priests today do not need to believe any differently from lay people who believe as they do because they have no alternative. Let us have a fraternal faith, sharing in the crisis of faith today; let us become involved in whatever storms faith today has to weather, for they too are sent from God. Then our message will be credible and acceptable and can be an example which gives strength to others.

What I have tentatively suggested above about a fraternal faith is also true of our relations with those who think they do not believe and those—the distinction between the two groups is not wholly clear—who really don't believe. If Christ redeemed us by suffering in himself a world empty of God, then the priest's fraternal faith must include the sharing of the contemporary crisis of faith. We cannot believe in the only proper and ultimately certain way which is required of us today, unless our faith is anchored in our time in the spiritual climate of our age.

It would be foolish and ridiculous to see the real or apparent loss of faith today, the contemporary crisis of faith, as being simply the result of human malevolence. There are objective reasons for all this: the inevitable and intrinsically valuable pluralism of culture for one thing—though we may note that it is precisely Catholic, anti-fideistic teaching that culture should spring from several sources and not, that is to say, from revelation alone. This pluralism has brought with it a variety of spiritual doctrines and trends which it is almost impossible for the individual to come to terms with objectively and which, viewed subjectively, he cannot be blamed for leaving unresolved. In addition there is the increasing freedom from sociological constraints in fundamental questions of truth: this again in the final analysis is of positive value for Christianity since a real faith requires a personal decision and a personal freedom which have too often been compromised by such sociological links, whatever supporters of the "national church" idea or of a more or less moderate *compelle intrare* may say.

Finally there is another tendency, in itself proper and of positive value, but often not fully understood or integrated: the growing accent on the unworldliness of God, which is connected with fundamental changes in man's view of himself and the world today. These and many other similar reasons create a climate for faith which, although it does not justify the apparent disappearance of faith today, nevertheless makes it comprehensible and allows us to see it very often as a merely apparent reluctance to believe; a reluctance which, seen in wider historical perspective, is simply a critical adolescent stage in the faith of mankind and does not precede its decline.

What does this mean for us? As priests today we need a fraternal faith towards our apparently unbelieving brothers. How can we hope to be heralds of the Gospel for them, how can we be a fruitful example of faith, how can we share the agonies of their lack of faith and pray in Christ for the grace of faith for them—how can we do this if we act, in their eyes or even in our own, as though we were different from them?

We have the duty, the right, and the grace to see our faith in Christ as part of the same world that they live in, that made them what they are: an unimaginably vast world of science, continually developing; a world in which man is still searching for himself; a world of rational planning and technology; a sober rational world, where miracles do not happen every day; a world of hard and fast laws and precise calculations; a world without God, in which such elements of the miraculous as remain must be discovered and experienced afresh. They, like us, come from a world in which God's power seems almost always concealed behind the workings of the world itself, in which religion itself is subject to a thousand earthly laws, in which the inevitability and burden of death is felt as more immediate than the happiness of eternal life.

Our faith, too, must come from this world. If we are in truth men of today, if in our faith we do not run away from ourselves out of a mistaken and misplaced fear, then our faith will face up to our situation in the world of today. This situation must affect the form of our faith, penetrate it, purify it and test it, make it humble and modest, ready to face up to this one situation again and again. Our faith must be such that the so-called unbeliever cannot deny that there stands before him a man like himself, a man of today, who does not utter the word "God" easily or unthinkingly, who does not presume to have penetrated this mystery, a modest, coolly sceptical man of today like himself, who nevertheless—no, not *nevertheless—for that very reason* believes. Our faith must be seen by unbelievers to be a fraternal faith.

But if this were always and everywhere the case, how different the form of our faith would have to be. Not different for reasons of cunning apologetical tactics, but because we ourselves aspire to a full and pure Christian faith. We must overcome all the traits of an unfraternal faith in ourselves; that bogus tone of superficial conviction and manner of speaking in which the message of Christianity becomes an easy remedy for all the evils of the age; habits of mind and speech which suggest we do not feel the alienation from God which characterizes our age, but imply that we know everything, have understood everything, imply that Christianity is a formula which contains the explanation of the world rather than the grace-bearing commandment to abandon ourselves completely to the incomprehensible mystery of ineffable love.

It is not without value to warn against the dangers and misunderstandings in the writings of Teilhard de Chardin. But it would be still more valuable if theologians instead concentrated on building up a balanced faith on the basis of modern knowledge and experience. This does not involve an unconditional acceptance of the way in which our contemporary non-Christian world regards human existence. Indeed it can just as well involve a fundamental transformation of modern conceptions of life. But whenever warnings against diluting the Christian message take on a clerical tone of superiority, the tone which implies: we know all about this, all these new problems are basically either a muddying of permanent clarity achieved long ago or belong to the category of sciences which have no religious significance, then such warnings are completely unconvincing and ineffectual.

If we had a fraternal faith, always and everywhere the "unbelievers" would not so easily be able to suspect that we were ultimately only safeguarding ourselves and the Church and bourgeois values, rather than safeguarding them, our brothers, as well as ourselves, from the descent into the depths of despair or weary resignation. May God grant us a fraternal faith, a faith which is real and true in his sight.

Faith challenged

The second characteristic of faith today is closely related to the first: its frank acceptance of the fact that it is in danger.

Let us consider first of all that every age has its own particular task to fulfil and that it is not required of any one age to attain the same degree of achievement in everything. Each age must fulfil its own task so that all ages together will constitute one unique whole before God. It is theologically correct to say that faith, at any rate in the abstract formulation given by the Council of Trent, does not express the totality of the Christian way of life. But where a particular form of faith is truly realised, the rest, Christianity in its totality, is added of itself; and where the rest is lacking, it is an indication that faith itself, the foundation and source of life before God, is not genuinely and existentially alive.

In this sense we can say without hesitation that today faith is the special task and the special mark of Christian existence, to which all the rest will be added. When, through the grace of God, a man succeeds in experiencing God—this ineffable mystery which is present to us in ineffably merciful form in Christ and his grace, when he succeeds in opening his life to this infinity over which he has no control, and when he can abandon himself in the midst of his own disintegrating existence to this ineffable being, then through the grace of Christ faith is truly present. Where this is so, the characteristic mark of our present-day existential situation is fulfilled and we can be sure that all other things will be added to it: repentance, love, acceptance of the forgiveness of sins, and the more sociological, ecclesial, and concrete features of faith.

If, however, in the pattern of human and salvation history, faith today is an especial characteristic of our situation and our task as Christians, we cannot be surprised if it is exposed to dangers on all sides. There is no need to recapitulate the external reasons, already briefly indicated, for the fact that our faith is in danger. It is, however, important for us to see that this endangered state is an essential impulse of true faith and that the present crisis of faith, if we are to understand and come to terms with it properly, is a situation which the believer should, and indeed must, confront with courage and confidence. Only thus can his faith become validly a faith for today.

In dogmatic theology we talk comfortably, even glibly, of the fact that the certainty and stability of faith does not exclude the possibility of doubt or of losing it. Yet we are aware that this statement is difficult to reconcile with the character of faith as something absolutely secure, firm, and "demonstrable" by fundamental theology, and so we tend to regard the possibility of doubt as a regrettable and unpleasant—if inevitable—attribute of the pilgrim's faith. Such a reaction is misconceived, for it is only in this situation of risks and dangers that the pilgrim's faith, as a saving act given by God, can exist at all. Only in such a situation does faith form the ultimate basis of my very existence at its deepest level (otherwise it is not faith, but an unimportant piece of furniture, merely a part of my existence, the real basis of which is something quite different) and at the same time depend upon the ultimate free choice of my whole being. Only in this situation of risks and dangers is faith a unity (not an identity), a unity which reflection cannot disentangle and which combines the freedom of decision with the objective basis of man's existence.

We have no reason, therefore, to conceal from ourselves the fact that our faith is "at risk." On the contrary it is a striking feature of the particular form of faith required today that it must confront this danger consciously. There is no absolute contradiction here of the old, well-tried, traditional maxim which advises us to avoid endangering our faith unnecessarily (by irreligious surroundings, antireligious books, etc.). But the primary question today is how far it is possible for us to avoid such dangers and whether today we do not need to adopt different tactics to preserve our faith from those of earlier times, when a spiritual climate of homogeneous belief and certainty of faith was possible, such as is not possible today. To continue to act in the same way today would result in the kind of repressions which wreak a bitter revenge on us, rather than in the sensible avoidance of dangers to faith. Nevertheless there is unquestionably something of permanent value, even today, in the old maxim; but here is not the place to discuss it.

Let me repeat: this confrontation, this fearless and courageous acceptance, this realistic appraisal of the threat belongs to the form of faith we need today. Accepting the danger to which our faith is exposed means admitting that the individual priest and theologian of today cannot produce a positive, direct, universally satisfactory, and "scientifically" objective theological proof of the credibility of Christian revelation for himself alone. The demands of the separate areas of knowledge involved are too great, the methods too complicated and too difficult. As an individual he cannot demand for himself the sort of scientific basis for faith which would be satisfactory in the modern world, any more than the ordinary layman can, who manages nonetheless to believe. In addition to the perfectly valid tasks which it has tackled up to now, rational fundamental theology must develop a global indirect basis for faith to show why faith remains a rational and responsible matter, even though the individual is unable to sort out for himself all the problems of philosophy, religious history, exegesis, and the frontier areas between theology and science, which are objectively the concerns of a direct and positive fundamental theology. It is clear that this fundamental theology is by no means sufficiently developed and that the necessity for it is not sufficiently recognized.

To face up to the fact that our faith is at risk is to admit that our ability to believe inwardly is in danger, that the possibility of fulfilling our faith in a genuine way in our practical lives is often in danger of disappearing. How often we as priests replace a genuine faith by a theological and pastoral routine without really admitting it. Our faith, exactly like the layman's, is often in danger of becoming no more than a flimsy ideological superstructure with which we hide and dissimulate a fundamentally profane existence and attitude to life. Why don't we face up to this? Why is there so much suppression and "official" hypocrisy in this respect? If faith in God is a powerful act of grace performed within us, then we do not jeopardise the faith in us by praying and confessing: "Lòrd, I believe; help my unbelief!", or by admitting that in the last analysis it is not we, with all our ingenuity and all our theology, who keep our faith out of danger, but God. To see that our faith is imperiled is not of course a means to a complete cure for a weak faith, but it is certainly the necessary starting-point for such a cure. Only the man who has nothing but himself and his own strength must act as though he personally were invincible. As Christians we should not need to take this attitude, for we have God; it is precisely in our weakness that his strength becomes effective, even in the weakness of our faith, provided that we humbly accept this weakness and do not pretend that it is we who have the strength.

To admit that our faith is threatened means finally that we have both the knowledge and the practical experience that salvation grows out of danger. For, in fact, the real danger to faith today comes ultimately not from particular intellectual difficulties associated with science, exegesis, or the history of religion, such as threatened—at any rate in their reflective consciousness—the men of previous centuries. It is not a few isolated tenets of faith from among a host of other convictions which are in danger today, but faith itself: the ability to believe, the capacity for developing an unequivocal, comprehensive, and challenging belief and making it powerfully effective in our lives and throughout our lives.

What menaces faith today as a whole is the sense of vacuum, the deadly loss of meaning and purpose, the metaphysical lassitude, the apparently irreversible process of inner decay, the helplessness of the spirit against the powers of the flesh, violence, and death, the apparently senseless cruelty of history, the progressive crushing of defenceless truth by the brutality of so-called realism, the way we are engulfed by the petty concerns of everyday life, our consciousness of an ever-present pluralism, of divergent and irreconcilable attitudes to life, the sense—much more striking and oppressive than ever before—of the tension between the formulas of faith and faith in action, the awareness—which is quite genuine and must be honestly accepted—that the actual form of our formulas of faith has its origins in an age with a mentality very different from our own.

But if we recognize all this, if we unmask in ourselves those substitute interpretations of life beside and apart from the commitment to faith, those tranquilizers for life's anxieties which lie ready to hand and which we secretly indulge in;

if we really admit our frailty and confront the deadly vacuum, which threatens us, more radically than the most radical sceptic, with fewer illusions than the most confirmed positivist—then we shall have realized the real dangers threatening our faith. But we shall have done more: we shall have laid the foundations upon which we can build our faith in the only form in which it is really valid today. For today faith is only real where it is lived in full knowledge of this situation; and faith is precisely the absolute answer, and is seen as such, only where the question too is put in an absolute way, where nothing is without exception and *a priori* clear, meaningful, and unquestionable (as it was for the nineteenth century bourgeoisie before Nietzsche). For only in confronting the situation in this radical way can man fully realize that neither he nor the world is God and that neither alone has any numinous radiance in which he can bask in peace and quiet. Only then can man see that God is God, the incomprehensible mystery which demands a radical commitment.

This is where Christianity begins and ends; provided that, at the same time, we realize that this mystery is the forgiving, self-giving presence of God. But this can only be experienced in the grace and the saving message of Christianity, if the bottomless pit of our existence is not artificially camouflaged —which all of us, Christians and non-Christians, are very ready to do (for we are all sinners)—and if we face up with courage to the immensity of the danger and to the anxiety which it creates in us. Then we shall see the danger itself as our salvation, a salvation which comes from God alone.

The radical simplicity of faith

In emphasizing the radical simplicity of faith as its third essential characteristic today, I do not intend to defend fundamentalism, nor the simplified theology of the Enlightenment, nor yet the modernist reduction of the tenets of faith simply to religious feeling interpreted naturalistically. What I do mean is the whole, permanent, revealed Christian and Catholic faith, as it has developed through the history of revelation and of dogma. Nothing more than this. But precisely here we are confronted with the question and the problem of radical simplicity and unity in our faith and in our experience of faith. Why?

Let us ignore for a moment, though it might seem to help us in our enquiry, the traditional Catholic teaching on *fides implicita*. According to this doctrine, it is not necessary to have an explicit knowledge of the entire content of faith proclaimed by the Church; indeed it may sometimes be preferable to know only a little. In fact, the limitations of man's mind and heart are such that the essentials of faith have a better chance of being realized if faith itself is based on a few fundamental elements rather than a host of abstract concepts. Leaving this possible approach to the problem on one side, let us consider instead the content of faith, in all its developments and all its details, as it has been handed on to us in religious and theological teaching, a permanent treasure of unquestionable value. We are still left with the same problem. Why?

The courage to believe and the capacity for making faith meaningful in our lives presuppose today, more than ever before, that the content of faith is not seen as a vast, almost incalculable, number of propositions which, collectively and severally, are guaranteed, from outside so to speak, by the formal authority of a God who reveals himself. Faith built up in such a way is threatened by the modern questioning—itself formal and abstract—of the reality of divine revelation quite apart from its content. A formally abstract and extrinsic view of revelation and a dogmatic positivism in matters of faith cannot, in fact, hope to combat the present threat to our faith. Man's picture of God today is of a being too transcendental, too absolute, too incomprehensible, for him to accept that this God would have wished to instruct him by drawing from the inexhaustible treasure of divine knowledge an arbitrary collection of unconnected propositions, to which, had he so wished, he might well have added others; propositions which apparently have to be accepted blindly, since neither

knowing nor understanding them seems to have any significance for man's life as he lives it. Modern man's picture of
God and his experience of historical religion make it impossible for him to accept that apart from a very specific history,
such as that of Israel or the Christian church, or the generally unsuccessful essays of natural philosophy in the religious
sphere, man's search for the ultimate meaning of existence
should have produced no more than errors or unanswered
questions.

In consequence, Christian faith today can only be genuinely
and uninhibitedly acceptable, can only answer the real questions and the legitimate viewpoints of our time, if it show
itself to be the authentic supernatural revelation of God acting in history and be seen to be God's sole, total, and fundamentally simple answer to the sole, total question which
man asks of his own existence. The progress and the content
of revelation, its different stages of development in history,
must appear in their true and genuine unity and simplicity.
This is an enormous task which theology still has to carry
out. It is easy enough, of course, to talk in general terms of
tasks which have still not been tackled, but any more precise
reference to an unsolved or urgent problem merely seems to
upset ecclesiastical and theological dignitaries. Those who
cling anxiously to the peaceful atmosphere of earlier times
regard all the really important questions as having been solved
or explained away long ago and see those who raise them as
malcontents who are wilfully confusing settled issues.

The unification and simplification of theological statements which I have in mind, and which on the whole is still lacking, should not simply stop at presenting the unity of the objective content of faith in a clearer and more radical way than before. It should also work out, on a generous scale, a kind of maieutic process to show how in religious experience, where grace is present, the reality proclaimed through the official historical channels of revelation can be realized and experienced existentially from within. For grace is given to every man, and this absolute self-communication of the tri-une God does not lie outside existence lived effectively, consciously, and freely. Just as grace, however, cannot be understood objectively by individual reflection, neither can the individual's simple reflection on grace objectivize any particular development of Christian dogma clearly expounded in the ministerial proclamation of the word. The unified presentation of the Christian message should, therefore, offer a bold synthesis of our present-day image of the world and the basic historical situation of modern man: his caution, his common sense and realism, his distrust of big words, his feeling for the development and unification of the world, and his consciousness of the gulf between reality and high-flown sentiments.

Obviously, I cannot here attempt to suggest how such a task could be carried out. But perhaps I can very tentatively indicate some guidelines. To achieve this simplification in the presentation of dogma, we must realize that fundamentally there are only three absolute mysteries in Christianity: the Trinity, Incarnation, and sanctifying grace; and we must be aware of the internal relationships between these mysteries and especially of the essential unity of Incarnation and grace. We must grasp that this unity is already immanent in the trinitarian economy, since in Christ and his grace we have God's absolute communication to man. We must show that man is absolutely open, radically accessible to this absolute mystery of God; we must make sure it is understood, in the unity of the exterior message and the interior experience of grace, that this absolute mystery brings man absolute forgiveness and love by its complete and radical communication of itself; that God is not in fact remote, silent, and unheeding, even though he remains a mystery and only becomes real to us in this communication of himself. Finally it is essential that the *a posteriori* christology of Jesus of Nazareth should be joined to an *a priori* existential christology of the humanity of God, based on metaphysical anthropology. This christology would explain how God's absolute and definitive revelation involves the divinized humanity of the God-Man, and how the absolute savior and the definitive eschatological acceptance by humanity of God's self-communication necessarily leads us to the teaching of Chalcedon. If this were done, a great deal would have been achieved, in my opinion, towards a simplification of the dogmatic conception of the content of revelation. I am, of course, very conscious that what I propose may at first sight—but only at first sight—appear to be even more difficult to understand than traditional dogmatic statements.

What Christian dogma teaches over and above this lies on the social plane, the plane of historical accidents, of liturgy and cult. But our contemporaries are not worried by the fact that this absolute religion, historically the most highly developed religion, has great richness and complexity in these dimensions and carries both the inheritance and the burden of its past. They are conditioned to accept such historical facts without undue concern. If only the essentials of Christianity—everything in it that has been freely ordained and revealed by God—could be seen to be divinely simple and self-explanatory. Surely the one thing which man finds immediately comprehensible is that the absolute mystery of God is the foundation of his own existence and that the easiest and at once the most difficult existential act is the acceptance of this ineffably loving and forgiving presence. This is the essence of Christianity. The history of revelation is itself nothing more than this history, guided by God, of the progressive awakening of man's acceptance of God, whose self-giving reaches its objectively and subjectively supreme climax in Christ. On this basis man today could come to realize more clearly that Christianity is not one of many competing world religions, but the fulfillment of them all. Only if, in one and the same fundamental theological movement, contemporary man is made aware of all this, will he be psychologically and existentially able, in the concrete reality of his thinking, to accept the "proof" that God revealed himself absolutely in Jesus Christ and not in the other higher religions, however important these may be.

This is perhaps a good place to clarify my attempt at describing one of the essential characteristics of faith today or at any rate to present it in another perspective. In our own life of faith, in our prayers, meditations, and sermons, we often fail to see the wood for the trees, as far as the content of faith is concerned. For this reason, our knowledge of the really decisive, fundamental experiences of Christian life is neither precise nor profound. To find deeper existential roots for our faith in the real foundations of our existence must necessarily mean a simplification and concentration of the content of faith, not through rejecting or discarding particular propositions, but through gaining a new perspective on them, unifying them, and establishing priorities valid for our Christian life.

It is, for example, not easy to know what prayer is and how it happens. To overcome a feeling of existential disorientation, the feeling that prayer is nothing but auto-suggestion; to believe it is meaningful for a miserable creature to talk into the endless desert of God's silence; to grasp that the word "father" is not the projection into the infinite of childish, subjective concepts which aim at a prerational domination of his existence, but is authorized by a God who, working in everything, liberated his creatures to his own freedom and love; to do more than understand all this theoretically, to realize it existentially both before and after prayer, along with the renewal of all the natural prerequisites of meditation, the evocation of the deepest levels of our humanity—to achieve all this necessitates innumerable efforts, experiences, and new beginnings.

Yet instead of concentrating, in our own and others' lives,

on these fundamental, extremely simple aspects of Christian existence, on the simple objective realities, all-important in the world of faith, which are an essential part of these aspects, we rush into explicit forms of dogmatic development, on which modern man is quite incapable of basing his faith.

Sensibilities must be spared, and I must, therefore, refrain from comparing the complications of modern theology with the simplicity of the Christianity it is ultimately talking about. Let me illustrate what I mean by an example. Suppose a priest were given the task of explaining to a layman—not a nun or a pious old lady, but a realist or positivist, an engineer or a professor of science, for example—that he, this engineer or professor, had already experienced supernatural grace, that he necessarily continues to experience it, and that this mysticism is one of the normal and natural things in Christian experience which no one can avoid, even if he overlooks it or cannot understand it or sets it aside as something he does not want to think about. I should be prepared to bet that the majority of the clergy would give up the task even before starting, indeed before they had even faced up to the obviously open question of how far such an attempt could in fact have any success with the engineer or professor.

I would almost be prepared to bet that many of the clergy, if they were honest with themselves, would have to admit that they themselves had never had such an experience, that the world of faith was something that had been taught to them from "outside," full of concepts bearing no relation to reality. By this admission, these members of the clergy would prove, not that they had in fact never had such an experience (God forbid!), but that the religious life of grace as the foundation of existence is as much a mystery and puzzle to them as it is to the majority of laymen. For most laymen a Christianity which is extrinsic and conceptually pluralistic, which is present as grace at the very foundation of their existence but of which they are not fully aware, can scarcely be anything more than a system that has been learned, a weak ideology which disintegrates in the cold and brutal realities of everyday life, unless it is propped up from outside by tradition or sociological structures and continues a superficial existence. And even for us priests, if you will pardon my frankness, such a faith would merely eke out an existence, sustained simply by the psychological and sociological conditions of our clerical vocation, which are no different from those of a non-Christian priest.

If the objection is raised that behind this institutional Christianity and its purely conceptual teachings which survive in spite of everything, we can discern the all-powerful grace of God supporting the faithful and their priests—then I can only ask that this obviously right answer be logically followed up. For this grace will then be seen to be the grace which, even unconsciously, we truly experience, that grace which through God's universal saving power is always and everywhere at work, the grace of ineffable, silent access to the mystery of God communicating himself in love and forgiveness. And this experience of grace, this indefinable "mysticism" of everyday life, will be seen to be the essence of Christianity and therefore one of the starting points of fundamental theology. If this experience is deliberately and consciously invoked, our conceptual and institutional Christianity, which of course is and remains something essential, will for the first time be realized in its true simplicity and unity.

The transcendency of faith

I hope you will not be put off by the title I have given to the fourth characteristic of faith today, nor by the fact that it is to some extent only one aspect of the third, which I have just discussed. What do I mean by the transcendency of faith in its contemporary form?

For any theistic philosophy or theology it is an accepted fact that God is infinitely superior to anything else in existence and to anything that can be imagined, and that any similarity, however great, between him and a creature contains intrinsically an even greater dissimilarity. But we cannot deny that this absolute transcendence of God is realized existentially with very varying degrees of clarity and intensity in the religious life of the individual and in the history of man's ideas about God.

The absolute incommensurability of God, the impossibility of reducing him simply to one element in man's universe so that man's horizons fix God's limits are ideas which have never really taken root in devotional practice. This is not surprising, for this absolute God must at the same time become the concrete God of the physical, explicit, and categorical enactment of our spiritual life. But this concrete God is only an absolute God, a radical mystery, an incomprehensible abyss from which everything originates, if he remains God in all of our concrete, categorical, religious life: inconceivable, illimitable, the immeasurable measure, the incomprehensibly eternal presence.

Man today is acutely aware of the fact that only in this way is God for him really God. Strictly speaking, he becomes atheistic only when faced with a God who is nothing but an aspect of the human world, its summit or terminus. This is not the place to go into details of the religious and cultural reasons for this progressive distancing of God from the world, nor to show that this transcendentalization of the reflective consciousness of God, which took place in the course of the history of European thought, and the parallel secularization of the world have their roots in the nature and historical dynamic of Christianity and are basically in no way contrary to the true significance of Christianity.

Here I should simply like to say briefly that in our faith, in its concrete expression in our own and others' Christian lives, we must be more acutely and clearly aware of this vast historical process of transcendentalization. Only if we take this process into account, more clearly and more sensitively than is usually done, can we live our faith genuinely and without strain. If we look closely, and with a truly contemporary awareness of God's ineffable greatness, at the way we think and speak about God, it should not surprise us that we often seem unconvincing, to ourselves as well as to others.

A few moments' reflection will suffice to confirm how often we speak about God as though we were looking over his shoulder, as though we were his privy councillors—or at least his borough councillors! We talk as though he were merely a regent who has great difficulty in retaining power, rather than the God whose will is absolute and to whom everything is subordinate; the infinitely great power at work at the heart of nature and of history; the God who takes upon himself the responsibility, before which there is no possible appeal, for all the enormities in the history of nature and of the human mind, each in its own way; the God whose name is unnameable and who is answerable to no one for his decisions, from the joyful triumph of the highest angels to the death agonies of his tortured creatures on earth.

We need to think for a few moments about the overtones in our preaching of the pure truth of Christian dogma, of the overtones which we priests, because of habit or sloth of mind and heart, do not even notice, but which the ordinary man today takes to be part of the Christian message and which he rejects as impossible—the overtones inherent in our theological, eschatological, and moral statements. We are forced to admit that the concept which is reflected in such overtones (not in Christian dogma properly stated, but in the overtones from which it is insufficiently distinguished) is too primitive, too categorical, too unequivocally formulated in worldly concepts to seem credible to the man of today. It is no use protesting against this assertion by invoking the sublimity of the great theology of the past. The point is whether the average sermon, our seminary theology, and our actual practice of faith today really manages to avoid, as much as it should do in our present spiritual situation, this primitive categorization of God. As far as western Europe is concerned, we surely have good reason to doubt it.

To save our own faith, as well as that of others, we must be much more sensitive. When we talk about faith, we should avoid giving the impression of being better informed about God's absolute mystery and his intentions than is ever possible for a man, even with God's help. Our theological statements must be seen to overcome narrow-mindedness and human prejudices and finally lead men not to the formulas of faith but to the mystery of God himself, who surpasses all understanding and who, in the peace which he offers us, has already overcome and reconciled, from first to last, the dialectic of divided, finite realities. We must talk in such a way that our words do not simply express concepts and propositions but, as the powerful word of the Gospel, bring, beyond the words themselves, the gift and the acceptance of God himself in his grace. All this may well appear to be very abstract. Unfortunately there is no time here to quote examples which would prove how often the idea of the transcendence of God is missing from our actual faith and from our theological thinking today. But for those who are interested, examples are neither rare nor difficult to find.

The importance of the transcendency of faith today has another aspect. If 'God' does not mean a reality situated in the world and in the field of human experience—a reality which is greater and more influential than others, but still only one among many—but is instead the foundation and the horizon which encircles everything without itself being encircled, which is in control of everything without itself being part of the larger universe, then it is due to the fact that God is always the objective (without this implying any ontologism) of the unlimited transcendence of the human mind, the incomprehensible and illimitable objective which makes possible the confrontation between the mind and the realities of the world.

This in no way contradicts the possibility, indeed the necessity, for proofs of the existence of God and for the reflective conceptual picture of God which results from them. God does not therefore appear on the horizons of human understanding first and foremost as a purely external object, which was not previously there. On the contrary, he is already present in human existence, silent and hidden, as the infinite, supernatural, asymptotic goal of the spirit, conditioning everything, including the processes of the human spirit.

Since the message of faith teaches us that the transcendental presence of the infinite mystery (that is, God) is also the source of a possible movement (by means of God's free communication of himself which we call grace) towards a direct vision, it follows that God is not only present in a silent and hidden form, but also as a giver of grace. He does not simply give himself, in an almost categorical manner, in the revelation of the word; he also gives the grace which divinizes the original essential transcendency of man at the source of his spiritual being. The question remains open whether man affirms or denies this supernatural existential of his life, whether he adopts his supernaturally exalted transcendency in trust and love, or whether he suppresses and rejects it and with culpable cowardice entrenches himself in the transient limitations of his own being.

Given this transcendence of God and the transcendency of the human spirit raised to the supernatural order, we must recognize that, despite the necessity for an historical revelation of the word, manifesting itself socially and authoritatively in the Church, our preaching is always directed at men who, whether or not they consciously know it, whether or not they want it, whether they accept or reject it, are men who are constantly being offered divine grace by virtue of God's infinite desire for the salvation of all. This grace, which is the self-communication of the triune God in that divine expression we call the hypostatic union, *is* fundamentally and ultimately what the message of Christianity (coming historically from outside) says.

We must be aware that we do not live among men who are pagans in the sense that they have experienced nothing of the reality of the Christian message and to whom we have the duty of bringing the reality of Christianity solely from the outside, with the help of our concepts, our stammered and often desperately inadequate words. On the contrary, we are faced with "pagans" who have received grace but who are not yet aware of what they are. This awareness necessarily reacts upon our own faith and is a vital aspect of the form of faith needed today—a transcendental faith. Our faith is made broader, more confident, and more patient. God's little flock does not live surrounded by ravening wolves but among sheep who may have gone astray and not yet found their way home, who may look like wolves from the outside but who may already have been or could be transformed inwardly, through God's grace, into gentle creatures of God.

A faith of this kind knows that God's kingdom and the power of his grace extend far beyond the words and the power of the church. A faith of this kind sees the unbeliever as a brother, who generally only thinks he does not or cannot believe, in whom grace is present even if not expressed conceptually, even if not completely free. Nonetheless it is there in the depths of his being; it comes to meet us and collaborates with us if we offer the historical and magisterial message of Christianity capable, in these circumstances, of bringing about victoriously a man's eternal salvation. It is effective even if, whether or not through any fault of our own, we deliver our message in such a way that it does not correspond to the saving grace already at work, perhaps unperceived, in the depths of his being.

A faith of this kind puts us face to face with a God greater than our mind, our heart, our words, our faith, and our Church; indeed it is the faith of the Church itself that God is greater than anything, greater than faith, greater than the Church. Greater here means more powerful, more merciful, more victorious; master of the paths we cannot find, merciful even when we cannot find a word of grace to utter, capable of entering through doors which we find closed to us today and opening them to the power of salvation. That is why, today above all, our faith is a confident faith: a faith which does not seek victory for itself or for us to enjoy, but seeks the victory of God. God wants us to believe in his victory, even in our weakness and our defeats.

A faith of this kind is patient, because it knows that God's apparent tardiness is a proof of his long-suffering and grace, rather than a judgment.

A faith of this kind can afford to speak discreetly and softly. For the God it speaks of does not fill the world and the hearts of men only through our strident propaganda. It knows it can calmly await God's good time and leave it to God to what extent his truth will find its expression in individuals and in nations in a form which we too can recognize.

A faith of this kind is not ashamed of the Gospel. In the mouth of the chosen and redeemed messenger it becomes a thanksgiving and proclaims the Gospel with modesty and courage, fully aware of the infinite difference between the words of the message and the reality they attempt to convey. For a faith of this kind knows that its words express both the secret aspiration and the ultimate sanctification of the man to whom the message is brought; that its words are only the divinely inspired and moulded echo, from the walls of the history of man's self-understanding, of that word which God has always spoken, as his own *Logos*, at the heart of man's being.

Why then should we not hand on this good news freely and confidently? If it is heard, it is a grace for us the messengers as well as for those who hear it. If it is neither understood nor accepted, then it is we who have been defeated; and we must consider the defeat as a source of power for our faith, for we know that it may please God to triumph through the weaknesses of his servants. We know that we need him, but that he does not need us. Our faith is assured of its future: it is none other than that which the infinite God, eternally young, promises to an aging world. Since God has eternity at his disposal, there is no risk of his coming too late.

What I have attempted here was not to describe faith itself, but simply to indicate some features of the form of faith appropriate for today and tomorrow; this is a different and a much more modest task.

But let me close by invoking faith itself and praising it. It is the faith of our fathers and of our own lives; the faith which was there from the beginning and revealed itself gradually through the history of man and of his salvation, until in Jesus Christ God's word and man's acceptance, ultimate reality and its expression, promise and its fulfillment found their absolute unity; the faith of the Church; the faith in which innermost grace and the austere and eternal word of the magisterium are united.

It is a faith which is quite simple, because it says only one astounding thing which is the one basis of our lives: that God is God, the eternal mystery we worship, which has given itself to us radically and directly, which we can lay hold of directly in our experience of grace in our own lives and see incarnate in history in Jesus Christ. It is a faith which is both the heaviest and the lightest thing in our existence: God's pure grace in our most intimate act of freedom. It is the faith which we confess and proclaim in our halting language, proclaim in the knowledge that God, as he promised by his definitive word in Christ, will never let us fall totally away from his truth, despite our stupidity, the narrowness of our minds and hearts, and the divisions of our history; the loving faith which justifies us, which is our strength while we live and our confidence when we die; the faith which can triumph even when we deny its existence; the faith which is given freely, but which we must ask for daily in our prayers and our temptations, since it is always a grace from God. In confessing our faith, we admit humbly that of ourselves we are cowardly, weak, and blind, unbelievers and men of little faith.

My brothers, let us close on a quiet note, so that God's gentle yet powerful word of grace within us is not drowned by our loud and weak human words. Let us pray: "Lord, help my unbelief," give me the grace of faith in Jesus Christ our Lord, in his Gospel and his saving power.

III INTELLECTUAL INTEGRITY AND CHRISTIAN FAITH

TRANSLATED BY WILLIAM WHITMAN

On reading the title of this essay, a hasty reader might maintain that "intellectual integrity" as a concept does not need clarification, the only question being whether it is a term one can use in connection with Christian faith. This is a question we will consider, but first it should be pointed out that the concept of "intellectual integrity" is not as clear as it may seem.

One might say that a person of intellectual integrity wants to get to the heart of things, that he is impartial in assessing the difficulties inherent in a universal viewpoint today, and that he is ready to accord intelligence and good will to a person of conflicting opinion. He has the courage to change his convictions at times, avoids fanaticism, and seeks "coolness" and "objectivity" in his decisions. He examines his own position just as critically as the position of others. He takes into account the prejudices which he may have acquired through the spirit of his time, his social class, his education, his own profession, yes, even through his own innate or social advantages, and feels constrained to do his utmost to overcome them and the ideologies that go with them. He realizes that truth may not be a very comforting thing, but may indeed be terrible. These characteristics, then, and this outlook describe a man of intellectual integrity. But if one earnestly aspires to intellectual integrity, then he must realize that all the dangers which these high qualities resist, do in fact take hold in the concept of intellectual integrity itself, twisting the person and corrupting him. Therefore it is necessary to state what intellectual integrity is *not*, what it cannot mean, so that the concept itself cannot be corrupted in turn by another ideological prejudice and its false authority. Two conditions, it seems to me, must be satisfied before one can speak of intellectual integrity.

Intellectual integrity and spiritual commitment

If a person has freed himself of the burden of spiritual choice or, better, assumes that he has freed himself of this burden, he *cannot* possess intellectual integrity. One is strongly tempted to assume that intellectual integrity applies to the man who is reserved and skeptical, who does not involve himself, and who makes no absolute decision. We see him examining everything but retaining nothing, although the Apostle advises us to do ·the contrary. He tries to side-step errors by avoiding all forms of real commitment. He takes the weakness of indecision—which each of us has at times, a temporary or partial condition which we ought rightfully to admit—and twists and turns it into a brave skepticism which will brook no illusions. No, this is not intellectual integrity.

Certainly, the man who in honesty and sincerity cannot go beyond a troubled atheism, who is downcast and sees only the

Medusa head of life's absurdity, should quietly admit this to himself, should try to accept this very experience with equanimity. For this experience too, so says the man of faith, God will turn into a blessing. But he must not maintain that his position is the only one compatible with intellectual integrity. How would he know? Who is to say that no one has ever come out of this purgatory, this inferno? How can he state that a person cannot find the strength to experience all this and still believe?

In any case, it is we who are damned to freedom or blessed with freedom, however one sees it—at this point it is still immaterial how this inescapable freedom is interpreted. It will have a hand in determining our final spiritual decisions and attitudes. There are no final basic attitudes, neither in the faith nor outside it, no tables of value or coordinate systems of existence which are achieved without the effort and daring of responsible freedom—not because blind, arbitrary action holds sway here, but because at this point insight and free action can no longer be separated. Thus it is that a person is not free if he maintains his freedom through skepticism, if he does not get involved, if, through a dreadful fear of falling into error, he will not respond to an insight in absolute terms; he ends up having struck the worse bargain. He lives, lives once, and sets up something that cannot be called back. He who attempts to live without making a decision, he who attempts to limit himself to a certain extent to the *bruta facta* of the biologist, he who steps up to the entrance to freedom and commitment and merely turns his ticket back in, in order to remain "neutral," is himself making a decision, and no one will grant that there are better grounds for this one than for any other.

Moreover, it is quite impossible to function in a dimension *this side* of a commitment. In fact, the attempt to remain neutral is nothing other than a refusal to respond thoughtfully to decisions that arise in the actual carrying out of one's life. For at least one commitment is inevitable (even if one thinks about it in a merely tentative way), and that is the decision to see life as an absurdity or as the expression of an unutterably mysterious meaning.

In short, *intellectual integrity requires that one summon the courage necessary to spiritual decision*, even when this decision is burdened with all the uncertainty, darkness, and fear of a mind bound to history and the finite, a mind conscious of its limitations but nevertheless resolved to commit itself.

But having said this, we stress our earlier contention, namely, that there are those who feel themselves duty bound to face many questions—yes, apparently the final questions— without an answer, holding the questions open with an utmost exertion of the spirit, but accepting no answers; such questioners do this in a sincere effort to satisfy their innermost conscience, their sense of responsibility to seek the truth. Let them; they must do this. The believer, the person who knows he is a believer, has only two things to say to this: first, that one man cannot look at another and tell where, by virtue of the second man's present location in the history of his existence, he may have decided against the holy meaning of existence, but by the same token the second man is not authorized to worship this meaning from a great distance because the first man must do so from the *same* distance; second, the believer will point out to the questioner that his stance is *already* a yes to the divinely blissful mystery of existence, and that he has not yet received the gift of courage to express to himself what his life in silent action already professes.

Intellectual integrity and theoretical reflection

There is a second pitfall to avoid with respect to intellectual integrity and the pursuit of faith, namely, the mistaken notion that true belief with true intellectual integrity requires one to think through all of the assumptions inherent in the faith, particularly the Christian faith, and to do this in a thorough, scientific manner. The belief in God as he expresses himself in rational concepts, the belief in Jesus Christ—in the story of his life and sufferings on earth, and the belief in the Church— all these taken together make up a vast store of facts, statements, and concepts which set forth the content and assumptions of our faith.

Intellectual integrity and faith would certainly conflict if one were only able to believe—and only allowed to believe— after one had made a careful "scientific" examination of these assumptions. Who could hope to accomplish such a thing in his short life span, with his limited scientific possibilities, despite his being a layman in a thousand areas? Who could be simultaneously a deep metaphysician, a religious philosopher, a religious historian, an expert in the intellectual, religious, and historical climate prevailing at the time of Jesus Christ, an exegete, a Bible theologian knowledgeable in the enormously complicated methods of modern research, a specialist in the situation linking a budding Christianity with the classical world in which it grew, a historian specializing in the tortuous paths by which current dogma and the Church have reached rational expression, an expert in the controversial theological problems concerning Christian faith and its history? Who could be all these things and be them *profoundly?* No one. Not even the individual theological specialist, because today, at least, stepping out of his narrow specialty, he is no more than a lay believer and a Christian with respect to the intellectual merit of his faith.

As basic Catholic theology pursues its normal course, it furthers this misapprehension. By nature, its task is to confront these fundamental problems, work them through, and justify the faith in rational terms—for the moment we put aside just what this comes down to. Now the individual Christian may, particularly if he is an educated man, make the dangerous inference that he should do the same thing, disposing of all the *praeambula fidei* through scientific thought. He assumes that educated folk, using a little good will and intelligence, should perform this task, giving particular thought to the religious stance of "the common man" who, he assumes, is naturally not expected to do this for himself. This notion has been tacitly implied rather than prescribed *in thesi* and does stand at odds with the educated man's exercise of intellectual integrity. Through firsthand experience with science, with its complexity, its vacillations, its disappointments and uncertainties, he knows that he cannot both perform this task and preserve his intellectual integrity. Having been subjected to the idea that responsible belief is contingent upon his performing, individually and subjectively, the objective task of basic rational theology, he concludes that he cannot believe and ought not to believe.

There are, of course, non-Catholic interpretations of faith. They allow faith to be irrational from the very beginning and limit its content to an area which we would consider inaccessible to rational reflection. Theories such as these presuppose that faith is a completely irrational stance and has nothing to do with intellectual integrity. The Catholic concept of faith does not tolerate such a simple way out. Catholicism holds that faith, in and of itself, has intellectual content. It is bound up with historical realities which are indeed open to rational inquiry. Faith neither wants nor can bring about a schizophrenic split in the logical, existential unity of the consciousness. Belief, if accepted in irrational and absolute terms, becomes ideology, becomes a dream in the otherwise concrete existence of a man who approaches his experiences rationally—a dream without power, except to people addicted to fantasy.

The Catholic perception of self requires faith to stand to account before the intellect's demand for truth; thus, faith broaches this question of intellectual integrity of its own volition. This does not mean that this integrity has been preserved when an individual believer does a thorough job, scientifically and subjectively, of what objective basic theology is supposed to do. This is a false assumption. In fact, one can and one may believe with a responsible and truthful conscience without working out all the objective praeambula fidei in a scientific manner.

Why is this? Because the spiritual essence of man is basically and irrevocably constituted in such a way that an appreciable existential gap—if one can put it this way—exists between the implications of his actions and the product of his scientific thought. Certainly man cannot build his existence exclusively out of the elements he has acquired through scientific thought, materials he has scrutinized in this particular way—let it be said, there are other ways as well. Since he knows this gap cannot be bridged, since he knows that his action is not merely the outcome of his rational thought, he is justified and even obligated to accept this gap; he should, moreover, decide to take material which has not been "scientifically authenticated" and accept it—in our case, believe in it—in the day-by-day action of his life.

Naturally that does not mean that man is absolved from conducting reflective inquiry and criticism within the scope of his possibilities. Man must accept his existence trustingly and obediently, but his existence inevitably includes a zone of reflection and critical inquiry—one which he can certainly expand. Man is constantly facing an unanswered question raised by the answer of his very existence, a complete answer merely because he exists; here he must take a stand. But if one holds that spiritual existence should or could only be built out of materials approved at the inspection office of scientific inquiry, then one's scruples would be destructive, disabling, and contrary to intellectual inquiry.

I love my mother, with all that this implies, even though I have no theoretical certainty whatever that Mrs. So-and-so is really my mother. It is my acknowledged right and duty to make certain political decisions, to fight on one barricade instead of another, if it comes to that, even though I have no theoretical certainty about the objective correctness of my decision. Nowadays, sophisticated computers are put to work on problems such as these, but even they could not help me. This situation cannot be avoided by a declaration of theoretical, skeptical neutrality, for this in itself would constitute a decision with just as many consequences as would a clean-cut taking of sides.

The question, then, is how man may bear up under this terrible situation, this necessity for a decision from within the gap of his existence. The sensible answer is that this situation is *imposed* upon him, and the protest against it arises *within* this situation and does not go beyond it. Those who make their commitment in honesty and obedience are, as a brotherly group, and even if their commitments conflict, closer in loyalty to their conscience than are those skeptics who try to act out the politics of abstinence in the combat zone of truth. This is especially true when both are aware of the dark, bitter burden which any such choice carries with it. In the end, every responsible decision made by the conscience—be it of a material categorical nature—contains an absolute yes to the absolute challenging mystery of existence that we call God; thus he contains within himself the error committed by the pure heart looking to him for truth.

Of course, what we have just said about the existential gap *also applies to the relationship between intellectual integrity and faith*. In fact, it is particularly applicable here, for faith is principally concerned with an encompassing interpretation of existence, and Christian faith, as the proclamation of the historical occurrences regarding Christ's life on earth, makes statements about all the dimensions of human existence. In this case, the existential gap is necessarily widest when such statements and their authority, on the one hand, confront theoretical reflections which have been scientifically authenticated, on the other. A person who has *both* faith and intellectual integrity knows this, or should know and acknowledge this; he need not shy away from it. Of course, a person cannot hope to take the countless individual questions at hand, group them together, and through scientific reflection justify his faith in rational terms. But this is not what intellectual integrity requires us to do.

As a rule, we merely trust in the experiences of life, even when they are theoretical and not yet properly our own. Why can't we do the same here? One is aware, of course, of the historical, social, and psychological conditions which give his Christianity, his Catholic faith, a certain slant. One knows

CHANGE   #   5.02
TENDER CASH   #   20.00
TOTAL   #   14.98
SALE TAX @ 0.00%   0.00
SUBTOTAL   #   14.98
KUNRA N° CHIPS
5.99*   T 0 5.99 1898855013 #
CROSSING TO AVAL
8.99*   T 0 8.99 0960251092 #
02/08/94 14:40   M   0   8658

WATERSTONE'S

that there are innumerable people who are not subject to these influences. One can calmly admit to himself, "I probably would not be a Catholic if certain preexisting conditions had been different, if I had not been born and raised a Catholic."[1] One knows, and he can quietly admit that even under the best circumstances, a thorough examination of basic theology will not afford him absolute certainty in his attempt to justify his faith in rational terms, and that he is therefore continually experiencing the openness, changeability, and indecision of spiritual development.[2]

Intellectual integrity may require all this, but it certainly does not mean that faith degenerates into tired skepticism. Faith as such, as an act of the spiritual life wherein we embrace the word of God as the ultimate meaning of existence, must, if this faith is to be real, possess a free, absolute, and unconditioned nature. This nature is not contingent upon our examination and thorough acceptance of all the implications and assumptions of the faith, but stems from God—from his word and his grace. For it is simply there from the beginning, intact—or as a real possibility pressing toward realization. Thus faith justifies itself sufficiently at the very offset through what is inherent to it.

We put our complete trust in certain things as long as such things are not clearly untenable—this is merely a fact of life and is rationally justifiable—for we must give life a chance to justify itself, and it can do this only if we live it in openness and trust: because faith unlocks the gate to the infinite realms where meaning and mystery can step forward hand in hand

and dominate life; because one's sense of morality and truth—
to the degree that this sense embraces that meaning of word
and freedom which is responsible unto itself—requires that
the meaning of the unutterable mystery be relinquished only
within the context of a greater, purer, more encompassing
meaning; because the really daring faith knows that it is contained and nourished through the experience of grace; however discreetly, however anonymously this grace points toward
the quiet, serene freedom of God's mystery, it nevertheless
does bring its own testimony with it.

To reach a pretheoretical basic justification of faith we do
not need to see into the heart of all things in a positive
manner on this plane. We do not need to have an illumination
of life's meaning nor shelter in God's mystery—the "mystical"
experience of faith, if one will—merely with respect to the
"categorical" material which characterizes Christian and
Catholic faith. Intellectual integrity is not sacrificed as long as
the experience factually takes place and as long as this mystical
experience does not direct us, as concrete believers, away from
and beyond this "material." According to this view, we are
fully justified in placing our trust in a synthesis of transcendental mystical experience and the materials which make up the
Christian faith and in treating this synthesis as real and in
completing it in absolute terms within faith itself. This faith
carries its own critical faculty within itself. It inquires by itself
and asks itself the critical question concerning the conscience
in quest of truth.

But the critical reflective search for theoretical justification may have and should have a history and ought to take its time; it enters into theoretical questions and proceeds from those which life raises for the concrete individual in situations regarding his inner life and the history of his spiritual growth, questions which are so truly real and which offer us a real possibility to triumph over them. This true, critical attitude easily sustains questions which one can formulate "of themselves" but which do not necessarily existentially concern this or that particular concrete believer, for in all seriousness, modesty, and even courage the believer realizes, and must realize, that he is not competent to handle them. Each of us does not have to be a specialist at interpreting the Dead Sea Scrolls in order to believe with honesty. All honest believers do not have to dispute the *dernier cri* in research into Christ's life. It is strange how nowadays one tends to place everything man does on a historical continuum, even his sense of truth. Yet one will not trustingly accept his real history as a basis for the fulfillment of his existence. One maintains that history cannot contain a lasting absolute dogma of truth. But history itself demands this dogma, for it actually emerges from history, and without it there would be no true history.

We have tried to clarify the relationship between intellectual integrity and faith by seeking a clearer understanding of the concept "intellectual" integrity. Now we must look to the other side of the relationship and consider *the intrinsic meaning of faith.*

Christian faith as a whole

Faith, as the specific, complete, and fundamental fulfillment of human existence, is necessarily as complex and as deeply immersed in the mystery of God as is human existence itself. If our inquiry is to go beyond a simple affirmation of God, beyond an abstract or merely transcendental "theism," and focus on the very essence of Catholic faith, we must look to the "ultimate foundation" of this faith. Here the question is how and in what ways do the individual declarations of our faith relate to this "ultimate foundation"—objectively in the realities we are considering and subjectively when one accepts these declarations through faith. Vatican Council II clearly indicates that original tenets should be separated from those of subsequent derivation if one is to understand the faith.[3]

In the first part of our essay we maintain that a person of intellectual integrity may and must subjectively draw this distinction. One period in history differs from another; societies differ—and this too is a dimension of truth; there is also a difference between prerational fulfillment of existence, on the one hand, and rational metaphysical reflection on the other. These differences allow us to say that the Christian and the man need not reduce the sum of his faith to individual tenets which he must justify for himself alone, scrutinizing them one by one with his intellect. They also point up the fact that Christianity, by dint of the differences it contains, can only be accepted or refused as a whole. We will attempt to show that this whole can be accepted by a person of intellectual integrity.

To do this, we will first ask what this whole consists of. This is not an easy task, but one which is necessary, though in itself it does not lie in the main line of our inquiry. It is not easy because Christianity, at first sight at least, seems to consist of such an abundance of declarations, dogmatic and moral tenets, and assertions by the Church, that one can "hardly see the forest for the trees." In totaling up such an account it may seem that the number of figures which one is called upon to accept as a whole is so great that errors are inevitable, and that consequently one cannot accept the results in good conscience.

This attempt to reach Christianity's "ultimate nature" is necessary because one must perceive it as the whole that it is, particularly if he is simply unable to construct it synthetically, through theoretical reflection, out of its parts. Here again, independent of our main line of inquiry, Vatican II considers this comprehensive understanding a necessity, not merely in order to distinguish between the foundation of Christian revelation and the truths which go with it, but also to attempt a "brief formula" for the initiation of the catechumen: it maintains that the catechumen must understand that "freed from sin, he will be led into the mystery of God's love made known to him by Jesus Christ."[4]

Therefore, let us attempt such a *brief formula* and try to ascertain its relationship to intellectual integrity. We might say, "Christianity is the outward and socially expressed (through the Church) profession that the final mystery in absolute rule in and over our lives, a mystery which we call God, shares itself with us in the history of the free spirit, pardoning us and divinizing us; God's sharing of himself with us occurred historically, irreversibly, and triumphantly in Jesus Christ." I feel that this expresses the decisive element in Christian faith, expresses it in a formula which, if properly understood and developed, also brings out the further content of Christian faith, provided free positive statutes are not inferred from it, statutes which exist as such in the dimension of historical fact and which raise no particular problem for sober intellectual integrity.

The divine God as the mystery of human existence

Let us look at this formula in light of the assumption we have just made. The first thing that it has to say about Christianity and the Christian faith is that God is the unencompassable and incomprehensible mystery and should be recognized as this mystery. Christianity is not a religion which brings "God" into the equation of human existence, using him as a known integer as one totals up the results. It is rather a religion which sets man face to face with the Incomprehensible which pervades and encompasses his existence and makes it impossible for him to construct an ideology—concerning the ultimate nature of religion—wherein he maintains that there is a calculable root formula of existence which man himself can manipulate and out of which he can build existence.

Christianity is an emphatic no to all such "false gods" and wants man, without conquest and without presumption, to relate to God as the mystery beyond all words. Christianity knows that we only know God when we experience this mystery in quiet worship; its religious words are never final in and of themselves, for if they speak the truth, they are merely the last words we hear as we fall silent before the mystery; they seek to conserve it, to prevent its being supplanted by a concept of God. Christianity knows that this mystery pervades man's existence as the ultimate reality and the truth of truths, that in thought, freedom, action, and certain death the Christian will always go beyond the defined, reckonable, and manipulatable aspects of the individual things he encounters in science and life.

The Christian does not want to meet God as the defined particular within his existence, enclosed by the horizon of his thought and action, in which case God would not be God. He is involved with the living God who encompasses without being encompassed, who is an unutterably sustaining force, who throws us and all things open to question—to his question, but who is not summoned forth by our questioning. Rather, he is already there in that he makes the question concerning himself possible, implants in us the questioning impulse, while he himself remains beyond all question.

Christianity is not a castle of truth with countless rooms which a person must live in, one by one, in order to "enter into truth," but rather the one opening which leads one from individual truths—and errors as well—into the truth which is the one inconceivable vastness of God. But Christianity stubbornly and implacably maintains that one cannot encompass this brilliant, silent darkness surrounding one's life and pervading everything—namely this brightness and one's own darkness; one cannot steal away from this overwhelming thing, but must stand up to it, trembling with fear, determined to name it by its unnamable name, not adorning our false gods with its name.

But Christianity has more to say about this overwhelming, inexpressible mystery. For the moment it is a matter of no concern whether a person dares to hear this message from the deepest experiences of his pardoned conscience, whether he has the impression that it is the purified, fundamental impulse of humanity's religious history in which God's grace is secretly active, or whether he simply receives it as the testimony of Christ and the apostles. Christianity's real message is this: the Incomprehensible Element in our existence, encompassing us, causing us to suffer the limits of our finitude, although itself beyond this finitude, does not want to be merely our horizon. It is a horizon which, while maintaining its silence, arranges and directs our existence as a spiritual journey because, in creating a distance between itself and us, it makes possible "our return to ourselves" in knowledge and freedom and makes possible the incorporation of the environment of sentient experience as world and current age. It goes further and at the same time allows us to experience ourselves for ourselves as finite beings. The mystery we call God *gives itself* in its divine life in a real sharing of self. He is the grace of our existence.

We may consider creation to be God's establishment, in his "activity directed outwards," of the ungodly, yet this is only true in so far as the creation is a necessary medium which he creates so that he may share himself with us in ungrounded love. God is this ungrounded love, and his creation is the formation of a receiver to whom he communicates both himself and the finite world he established, distinct from himself. Thus he becomes the giver and the gift and the principle itself of accepting the gift, and thus the finite achieves completion of self—finite, to be sure—in God, the infinite mystery. The creator-created relationship is a necessary, indispensable structure of reality but not its essential content.

God creates because, in expressing himself, in divesting himself of himself, he wants to share himself with us; distance assures unity of love; creation, cohesion, and law—as the structure of the finite—assure boundless love; obedience assures God's freedom for us; distance from God makes the wonder more blessed and assures us that nearness to him which forgives us our trespasses. This is not so because a closer examination of the mystery would reveal what lay at its heart, but rather to assure the blessedness of the spirit which directly and ecstatically possesses the mystery, in order that, without thought to itself, it may love the one true light and life. This is the real content of Christianity, the unutterable nature of the absolute mystery which divinizes and pardons us as it gives itself to us, so that we might be able to bear up under it, accept it, accept it again and again through its act of sharing. In man's transcendental nature and history there are three aspects to God's sharing of himself with us; since this is his real sharing of *self*, these three aspects do properly belong to him and thus we find that his sharing of himself with us contains what we are accustomed to call, in Christian terms, his three-fold nature.

His sharing of himself with us, historically,
in the person of Jesus Christ

Jesus Christ is the foundation of Christianity and gives our religion its name. The mystery is closely bound up with him. The mystery of God's sharing of himself with us, in which he in his innermost majesty becomes man's absolute future, has a history; this is true because it is a free act initiated by God himself and because man is a historical man belonging to a historical humanity. It has a history since the final attainment of man's transcendental destiny, one which is divinized through God's sharing of himself with us, awaits realization in a historical context of time and space and in concrete encounters with a concrete world in which man lives and comes to understand his nature. God's sharing of himself with us—while being the transcendental innermost cause of the world and its history, its final entelechy—has a dynamism, a destiny to manifest in space and time, to unfold and move toward fulfillment. We call this the history of Christ's appearance among us, his life here on earth and his sufferings.

Our belief in the Incarnation of the divine Logos attains its fullest expression when this act of sharing reaches its greatest intensity, that is the irreversible phase where it is manifested as the divine offer and as a humanly free but divinely prompted acceptance. The dialogue between God and man enters an absolute yes on both sides, and man is this dialogue "in substance," a fully active participant. The dialogue manifests the absolute yes wherein man himself becomes God's yes to mankind, a yes spoken and accepted in absolute terms. This happens as soon as God's word is historically spoken and received in absolute terms. Of course, there are indisputable historical facts which indicate that this occurred in Jesus of Nazareth and is to be experienced in him. What we call "the Church," as the eschatological presence of God's truth and love contained in word and sacrament, is nothing other than the continuing validity of the historical fact that the history of God's sharing himself with us began in Jesus Christ, is believed in today, and continues to unfold in the present and future.

The correct understanding of theoretical statements

Does this mission, this view of man's ultimate nature, stand up under the scrutiny of intellectual integrity?

In answering this question, we should point out that these statements, speaking as they do to the whole of existence, are already extremely difficult to deal with in terms of linguistics alone. Taken as a whole, they do not have a discernible point of focus or internal structure. Their content is necessarily unclear for the very reason that they express man's absolute truth, as, of course, the original, undefinable mystery. This goes unnoticed by those who live in a spiritual sociological environment of a homogeneous kind, for through lack of comparison or challenge they cannot be aware of their own particular manner of stating things.

But today's world is highly differentiated; accordingly, we find all theological statements "inexact," complicated by

thousands of concepts, analogies, additional questions as to
their more precise meaning, all of them floating about in the
haze. But the threatening element in this language problem is
cleared up when we go on to make the discovery that the categorical content of all these statements speaks to this mystery
which lies *in* the haze. Only then do they find their true being.
If we read them with this in mind, then we are no longer
afraid of misunderstanding them, of finding that clarifications
fail to bring us to clear-cut conclusions. We do not wonder
whether the only man to focus on their true meaning is the
one who seems to take issue with them. They are pointing the
way to the lasting mystery which *is to remain* a mystery.

Of course, this does not do away with contention on the
plane of individual categorical assertions, for there are Christian realities in the realm of history itself, as there are also
correct and false, more or less complete expositions of that
movement—and its manifestation in history—which leads us
to God's unutterable self. But such contention has nothing
threatening about it once we realize that the formula under
fire can, without losing its force, lead the way to God's unnamable mystery. We discover that the truth of one's own
article of faith does *not* imply that another article of faith,
even a false one, could not be the concrete vehicle which
leads the other person to accept God's mystery in worship and
love. For we can easily make this point, even if the viewpoint
is somewhat unusual: Catholic teaching tells us that there are
both true and false articles of faith regarding religious realities;
false articles of faith arrived at through reflection endanger

salvation, but there are no false objectivized articles of faith which cannot coexist with the process of salvation ushering us into the truth of God.

The compatibility of faith and intellectual integrity

Let us assume that intellectual integrity requires one—and does not forbid one—to disassociate the fullness of reality and truth from the sum of realities and truths which one has experienced, examined, or otherwise dealt with. Let us assume that the mystery is not a peripheral phenomenon of one's intellectual existence, that is, not merely a leftover item which one has not yet come to grips with in the mind, but is rather the mind's steadfast foundation which it hastens to install in the mechanisms at its disposal. How, now, could intellectual integrity forbid one to believe in the transcendental experience of grace, in the mission of the Revelation contained in every experience? Can it deny that this holy mystery wants to give itself to us as the deepest and ultimate life, divinizing and pardoning us as it shares itself with us? Can it declare that the ultimate content of Christian faith is intellectually untenable? I hardly think so.

Much courage and grace are needed to embrace this faith which promises us the inconceivable height distinguishing man from a clever animal, particularly when one is dealing with the rational acceptance of this promise. But what authority, what criterion could indicate that such courage is untenable, lacks intellectual integrity, and is not a worthy element in faith? Every act of perception, every act of free will is a step toward the unutterable, the out-of-reach. Therefore, the only real question is whether the enormous span of possibilities which we ourselves cannot encompass lies eternally empty or whether it is filled with God's sharing of himself with us through boundless love. Isn't it our duty, therefore, to allow God to be greater than our meager hearts, to yield to both of them, so that neither will suffocate in our finiteness, to believe that God can and wants to come to us, and we to him?

The credibility of the dogma of the incarnation

We now consider intellectual integrity with respect to Jesus Christ, that is, to the last radical manifestation of divine sharing of self with our created spirits, in other words, to the final categorical definition of Christianity. There are two things to be said in this connection.

As for the "idea" of a God in human form, the teaching regarding the Incarnation of the Logos in our human existence, is, as "idea," acceptable to a conscience seeking to maintain its intellectual integrity. The conditions are: that man realizes that he himself is a being which is always transcending himself in the mystery of God, a mystery which shares itself with man; that man realizes, as indicated earlier in passing, that the idea of a God in human form implies an eschatological culmination in the historical process at the point where God shared himself with us—as its asympotitic goal, at least. Then too, the idea should be protected from mythological misinterpretations; the man in which God manifests himself is not a passive puppet, not a servant through which God expresses himself, not a new approach through which God, as savior, tries to correct mistakes he made when creating the world.

The God-Man is truly man, at a prayerful distance from God, free, obedient, subject to the development and the historically conditioned nature of man, even in his religious experience, since closeness to God, autonomy, and being increase in like rather than inverse proportion to one another. The God in human form is not a second and now categorical intervention of God the Creator, but the culmination of a story involving World, Spirit, and Salvation, a culmination toward which this entire history flows, through God's transcendental sharing of himself which began in the beginning and determined all moments of history, a culmination redeeming the debt of freedom. The Incarnation continues to be a mystery of God's sharing of himself. Seen under this light, it disassociates itself from unsuitable mythologizing; while it does not force the man of intellectual integrity to say yes to it, it is none the less credible and worthy of belief. Thus, the believer and the man with an objective sense of history are not disappointed, but rather recognize that the Incarnation is a quiet, unobtrusive process. The New Testament, if we read it correctly, testifies to the fact that man is divinized through grace in the course of his mean day-to-day life; it testifies to this fact in a marvelous way as long as one looks upon this existence with the eyes of a person wanting to believe.

It is essential that this "idea" of a God in human form is

reality for us, in and of itself, in the person of Jesus of Nazareth at this point in time and space. This is the message of a
historical fact and a constant source of annoyance to man,
who, in his transcendental pride, is tempted to declare that a
"historical truth" cannot possibly be the foundation of his
existence. But the man of intellectual integrity, conscious of
his own limitations, is aware that theories about history cannot
replace history itself. He knows that a concrete history which
is never fully plumbed by reflection is the necessary vehicle to
man's transcendent spirituality and freedom, so that through
faith in the finite world bound by time and space one comes
to know the eternal in the abstract and in himself. There is no
substitute for this courage to trust in the concrete.

Admittedly, one does not easily come by a scientific exegetic
proof that Jesus considered himself the metaphysical son of
God as Christian dogma has it. Proof of this kind is sought by
a person who can read, interpret, and translate, and who does
not have to have Jesus speak in the formulas of theological
metaphysics to understand what they mean. For a person of
this sort, such proof is not necessarily out of the question. But
while this method would be difficult for the concrete individual in light of his limitations, it is certainly not the only
method which intellectual integrity can bring to bear on the
question of Jesus' identity and the authentication of this identity. If the idea of a God in human form is a credible one, if
spiritual history derives sufficient courage from Jesus himself
to support the living reality of this idea, if one does not build
up his existence in a test tube but rather comes upon it and

trustingly gives it the chance to validate itself and to sustain, if one finds himself congregating with souls who believe in Jesus and who find God in him, then why should he hold back? What further justification do we need?

Intellectual sincerity and belief in the resurrection

Let us suppose that we find man an indivisible unit and a whole and that we cannot live without fulfilling our existence in terms of meaning and salvation; let us suppose that we believe in "the resurrection of the flesh," seeing it as the formula which expresses man's absolute future, that we do not dismember him platonically first and do not demand to know how we should think of man's final completion in total "transfiguration"; let us suppose we consider Jesus' life and death from this point of view. Now what compelling argument could an intellectually sincere man put forward to cause us to withhold our belief in the experiences which Christ's disciples had regarding Christ's Resurrection, which was hardly a return to *this* existence? Why should we doubt his resurrection and the two-thousand-year-old story of faith, power, and light? The skeptic is not the only one to know that the resurrected Christ, as he appeared to the disciples, is and must be incommensurable with the normal order of time and space. The believer realizes this too. But the fact that we cannot incorporate his Resurrection into the normal world of space and time does not mean that we deny it.

It merits our belief as long as this incommensurability is not regarded as mythology, as long as the Resurrection—as experienced by us as individual persons—has a lasting validity which binds us finally and concretely, in our existential situation, into reciprocal accord with the disciples. Seen in its true light, the Resurrection is the real revelation of Jesus' role as savior and not merely a marvelous, outward indication of this role. Thus, it combines with Jesus' own interpretation of his identity to form a unity worthy of our belief.

Here we must bring our reflections to a close. We realize that many problems have gone untouched. We have not considered intellectual integrity with regard to the socially palpable reality of Christian faith which we call "the Church," together with its claims to truth and moral instruction. We might point out, however, that in this day and age when man's social obligations are steadily increasing, it would be anachronistic and overly-individualistic to maintain that one could or should protect and personally realize Christianity's ultimate "ideals," while at the same time side-stepping the historical and social tangibles in which these "ideals" are historically given in concrete life.

My point is this: if one does not want to make an idol out of "intellectual integrity," if he does not maintain that the skeptic is less likely to fall into error than the believer, if he does not assume that noncommitment in theoretical matters is possible in the action of his life, then intellectual integrity certainly does not prevent him from believing, from risking his life on the reality which Christianity contains and confesses to. This noble virtue does not compel us to make decisions, it empowers us to make them, for it too comes to possess its final and only meaning when it courageously attains completion, beyond all traces of intellectual caution, in the mystery of existence and in love.

Notes

[1] A person can calmly recognize the historical contingency of his own faith without maintaining thereby that there are no grounds "in and of themselves" which "in and of themselves" lead one to Catholicism and without challenging the possibility that another person may begin as a non-Christian and a non-Catholic and become a Christian and a Catholic.

[2] The absoluteness of one's acceptance of faith hardly carries over into absoluteness in his rational justification of the praeambula fidei as such.

[3] On this point, see Vatican II Decree on Ecumenism, no. 11.

[4] On this point, see Vatican II Decree on the Missionary Activity of the Church, no. 13.